Titanic
The Ship of
Dreams

Titanic
The Ship of Dreams

John Harper of the *Titanic*

Robert Plant

CF4·K

10 9 8 7 6 5 4 3 2
Copyright © 2011 Robert Plant
ISBN: 978-1-84550-641-4
Reprinted 2012

Published by Christian Focus Publications,
Geanies House, Fearn, Tain, Ross-shire
IV20 1TW, Scotland
United Kingdom
www.christianfocus.com
email: info@ christianfocus.com
Cover design by Daniel van Straaten
Cover illustration Brent Donoho
Printed and bound in Denmark
by Nørhaven

Author's Note: The Collings and the Harrisons are based on real people who sailed on the *Titanic*. The Courtneys and the Harts – their names were changed because descendants of these people may still be alive. Other names have been kept unaltered. The events surrounding the final hours of John Harper's life have largely been taken from eye-witness testimony. Some incidents described on board the ship are from the author's imagination. However, though they are fictional, they are based on historical information and accounts of what it was like to be on board the *Titanic*.

Contents

Sailing Day

'Oh, Daddy, am I really going with you to America this time?' asked a wide-eyed six year old girl dressed in a knee length blue coat. Her curly locks of brown hair fell out from beneath the knitted-cream tam hat she was wearing. She gripped her father's hand tightly as they waited at Waterloo Railway Station.

'Yes, my dear,' answered her father beaming down on her. They were watching a train trundle into the station. It screeched to a slow halt as a cloud of steam enveloped its engine. 'Yes, Nana,' he repeated. 'You are coming with me and you will be staying with me all the time that I am in Chicago.'

'Oh, Daddy, I am so excited,' the little girl said as she bounced up and down eager to enjoy every minute of this great adventure she was about to embark on.

It was nearing 7.30 on the morning of Wednesday, 10th April 1912 and Mr John Harper, a Baptist pastor, and his daughter were waiting for a special train known simply as the *Boat Train* to take them to Southampton from where they would sail to America.

One by one, the doors of the train's carriages were opened and passengers clambered out onto the station platform. Soon it was filled with people pushing, pulling and carrying suitcases and trunks of all shapes and sizes. Nana and her father managed to make their way through these passengers towards the empty carriages. 'Let me help you up, child,' the loving father said as he bent down and lifted his daughter into the train. With Nana safely inside, John Harper lifted their two brown leather cases into the compartment.

The carriage they had entered comprised of eight seats on either side with another door on the opposite end. This was closed as it led directly out onto the tracks. Nana's father carefully lifted both cases onto a shelf above the seats before making sure his daughter was seated comfortably. Nana chose the seat right next to the door. This allowed her to peer out through the window and observe the mass of people bustling about in the station. She stared open-mouthed as a porter escorted a lady, in the most amazing green velvet dress, towards their compartment.

'But I always travel first class,' the lady was protesting to the red-faced porter as he lifted her suitcase in at Nana's feet.

'I am very sorry, madam,' he responded, 'but the first class train does not leave for another two hours. If you want to wait for that you can, or else you need to get on this one which, as you have been told, is for second and third class passengers. It will take you, just like the first class train, to Southampton to join the new ship the *Titanic*.'

'I was never told there were two trains running today,' the lady continued to protest, 'but I am certainly not going to wait around this filthy station any longer. It really is disgraceful.'

The lady haughtily lifted herself into the carriage where young Nana and her father were sitting before turning to the porter again and exclaiming, 'When I am on the *Titanic* I am certain I will not have to wait to travel first class!' The lady then attempted to lift her luggage onto the shelf opposite Nana and her father.

'Here, let me help you,' John Harper spoke kindly. He stood up and took the case from her hand and lifted it up onto the shelf. 'They do make these shelves rather high,' he commented.

'Oh, thank you,' the lady said, her voice softening a little from the harsh way she had been complaining to the porter.

'It's my pleasure,' Nana's father said as he returned to his seat.

The woman stood rearranging her dress before taking a seat opposite Nana.

'I couldn't help but hear that you are travelling to New York on the *Titanic,*' John Harper spoke up. 'We're booked on that ship, although we will be going on to Chicago,' he continued pleasantly.

'I am going back to our home stateside,' the new passenger replied. 'My husband is a banker here in London, but we have a large apartment in New York. I always travel first class, but they didn't tell me there were two trains running to Southampton today, otherwise I would have arrived at the station much later,' she continued with an indignant air about her.

'What's New York like?' quizzed Nana, her eyes still staring at the velvet and brocade dress the rather well-to-do lady was wearing.

'Oh, it's just amazing,' the lady replied, putting heavy emphasis on the word amazing. 'In fact it must be the most exciting place on earth!' she continued beginning to lose her haughty countenance as she smiled easily at Nana. 'There are big shows on every evening in the theatres, and restaurants that open all night. There are candy stores and street entertainment on just about every corner. It really is an exciting place. You must get your mummy and daddy to let you spend some time there!'

'Mummy is in heaven,' Nana answered quietly. 'She went there when I was born so I don't remember her at all.' The girl's voice was calm as she spoke of the loss of the mother she had never known. 'But I do have her photograph here in this clasp,' she continued, her manner brightening as she opened a little silver locket and showed the photograph to the lady.

'Oh, I ...' the lady blushed with embarrassment, 'I ... um didn't mean to be ... um ... I'm sorry about your mother,' she finally managed to get out.

'That's alright,' Nana answered. 'I know that she is happy in heaven with the Lord Jesus.'

The lady pulled herself forward towards the little girl and said kindly, 'I am sure she is.' Then turning to Nana's father she lowered her voice and said, 'It's lovely when they are at the age to believe in such things, isn't it?'

'To believe in what things?' John Harper answered simply.

The lady leaned closer to Mr Harper and lowered her voice even further, not wanting Nana to hear, and said, 'To believe in heaven.'

'That's not some childish fantasy,' replied Nana's father. 'Not at all. It's a very real and wonderful place that God has prepared for those who trust his Son as Saviour.' The woman looked across at the man in a puzzled, but thoughtful expression. 'You see,' he continued, 'I am a preacher of the gospel on my way to Chicago to take meetings in the Moody Church. There I will tell people about the love of God, the Lord Jesus Christ and the way to heaven.' He paused as he looked at the woman who appeared to be listening with interest to what he was saying.

'Have you been to America to preach before?' she enquired politely.

'Yes, I was there at the end of last year. This time they have asked me to stay for three months and I am pleased to be able to take my daughter with me. We were supposed to be travelling on the *Lusitania* from Liverpool last week, but our plans changed and now we intend travelling second class on the *Titanic*. So as I am sure you can imagine, my daughter Nana is very excited at the prospect.'

'Moody's Church,' she repeated thoughtfully. 'That must be named after D. L. Moody, the American evangelist,' she enquired.

'The very same,' Nana's father replied, glad to be able to continue the conversation.

'Interesting. I heard him about twenty years ago. He preached, and a man whose name I forget sang.' She paused before adding, 'A beautiful singer he was too.'

'That would be Ira Sankey,' Mr Harper answered. 'Moody and Sankey had various meetings here in the United Kingdom and many people trusted the Lord Jesus as their Saviour during that time.'

'I heard Mr Moody preaching, but I wasn't convinced about the sin business and my need of Jesus as my Saviour. You see I just didn't really understand why I should want this man called Jesus, who died so long ago. Anyway,' she continued, 'I don't believe I have really got any needs. I can have just about anything I want!'

'You may be able to have everything you want, but madam what you really need is a Saviour,' Nana's father added.

'Whatever do you mean?' the lady answered taken aback by Mr Harper's bluntness.

'Well, so many people miss their greatest need of the Lord Jesus as their Saviour because they fill their lives with other things that they consider to be of more importance. The Bible says, "How shall we escape if we neglect so great a salvation".'

The lady moved her gaze to the window as a guard closed the carriage door and walked on up the platform. A few moments later they heard his whistle blow and felt a judder as the train started to pull away from the station.

They moved off so slowly it seemed that the engine would not be powerful enough to pull the endless snake-like length of carriages. Nana watched the long platform as it slid gradually down the length of the train. Soon it was gone and the train whistled as it trundled along Waterloo Bridge over the River Thames. As the occupants of the carriage looked across the river they could see the clock tower of Big Ben in the distance and sitting behind it the impressive buildings of the Houses of Parliament.

Mr Harper smiled at the lady and pointing across towards Big Ben said, 'The Bible says, "It is time to seek the Lord." People seem to be able to make time for many other things, but not for God.' The lady looked thoughtfully out of the window, watching the skyline of central London pass slowly out of sight.

Gradually the train started to pick up speed and it soon seemed to Nana that they were almost flying through cuttings and over bridges. As they passed through the outskirts of London the railway was bordered by the gardens of Victorian town houses. These gardens were just coming to life in the spring sunshine. Nana looked on in delight as she saw trees breaking into bud fly past the carriage window along with clumps of daffodils and primroses. The flowers brightened up the green grass of the railway line embankments with their vibrant yellow colours.

'Do they have trains in America?' she asked her father innocently.

'Oh, my dear,' the lady answered, as she laughed out loud, glad for an opportunity to change the conversation. 'They have trains ten times bigger and ten times faster than here in England!'

'Do they really?' Nana replied as she looked away from the window and towards the lady's smiling face.

Nana's father interrupted, 'They do tend to be bigger and perhaps a little faster than those here, but maybe ten times is a bit of an exaggeration. Would you not agree, madam?' he said with a rather roguish smile on his face.

The lady shifted a little uncomfortably on her seat, 'Perhaps so, but they are a bit more comfortable!'

'Yes,' Nana's father laughed, 'I'll agree to that. They certainly are more comfortable than most trains I have been on here in Britain.'

'Now that we are on speaking terms,' the lady suggested, 'I think that it is time we got to know each other properly. My name is Margaret Smithers.'

'I am very pleased to meet you Mrs Smithers, and my name is John Harper and this is my daughter, Annie Jessie, but I just call her Nana.' Mr Harper ran his fingers through her tousled hair. 'As Nana has already mentioned, my wife, Annie, passed away when she was born. I gave Nana my wife Annie's name, but somehow over time it has been changed to Nana. So you see I have to try and play the part of both father and mother. I am not sure that I do a very good job of either.'

'Oh, no, Daddy,' Nana responded with enthusiasm, 'You're the best daddy in the world and I never want to leave you, not ever.'

Mrs Smithers laughed, 'I am sure that he is indeed the best daddy in the world and if I'm not mistaken I think he may have a slight Scottish lilt to his accent?'

'Yes, that's right,' Mr Harper answered.

'So whereabouts do you come from?' Mrs Smithers asked.

'I'm from the west side of Scotland from a little village that I am sure you will never have heard of, called Bridge of Weir.'

'Yes, you're right. I haven't heard of it. Do you still live there?'

'No, I have not lived in Bridge of Weir for a long time. I was a pastor in Glasgow for some years and then God directed me to move down to London about eighteen months ago. We now live in Denmark Hill in Surrey, where I am pastor of the Walworth Road Baptist Church.'

'Did you say that God directed you to London?' Mrs Smithers questioned with a touch of scorn in her voice.

'Yes I did,' Mr Harper replied with earnestness.

'How does God direct you, does he speak to you from heaven?' she continued in a mocking manner.

Mr Harper continued calmly, ignoring her tone of voice. 'The Bible tells me that if I "acknowledge him in all my ways, he will direct my paths". So I know that if I pray to God and read my Bible he will guide me as to what I should do and where I should be. I also know that my life will be happier, because God knows what is best for me far better than I do.'

Mrs Smithers looked away before replying, 'I do admire your belief in God, but I am not sure that I want or need a faith like yours. I have already stated I am very content and have everything I need.'

'Maybe you do think you have all you need for this life, but what about the next life?' Nana's father continued. 'You see, Mrs Smithers, you never know when danger and disaster are near. What if something untoward happened on our journey to New York? I have a certainty that should I die today then I will go to heaven, but what about yourself? What will happen when your life ends and you are parted from your money, gold and treasures?'

Mrs Smithers squirmed uncomfortably in her seat unable to answer the pastor's searching question. She turned again to the window as if something had caught her eye.

The train had now left the towns and villages and was taking them through the gently rolling South Downs.

The next part of the journey passed very quickly. Mrs Smithers took her smelling salts from her matching velvet bag then closed her eyes as if she was trying to get some rest. Mr Harper himself had a nap while Nana sat with her face pressed against the window.

The greens and browns of the countryside were eventually replaced by houses and other buildings as the train began to pass through what was unmistakably the outskirts of another large city.

'Daddy, Daddy,' Nana's little voice broke excitedly through the stillness of the carriage. 'We are slowing down. I think we are here. I think that we are in Southampton.'

Mrs Smithers opened her eyes and exclaimed, 'Oh, yes, indeed we are. This is Southampton. We will soon be at the docks and then hopefully we'll pull up almost alongside the *Titanic*.' Mrs Smithers sighed, 'I do hope that they have a porter on hand to help me with my cases.'

'Daddy,' Nana enquired excitedly, 'Will we have a porter to help us with our cases?'

'Oh, no, precious one,' her father replied, 'We will just manage the cases ourselves.'

The train chugged through the city and Nana continued gazing out of the window with great interest at the houses, parks and factories that passed on either side. The scene changed again as they crossed over a road where several horses and carriages laden with luggage waited impatiently for the noisy locomotive to pass by. Then almost as soon as they had crossed the road, Nana caught sight of it. Having never seen a ship before the little girl was almost speechless as she looked in amazement at the colossal vessel that came into view on the right hand side of the train.

'Is…is…that…it…Daddy?' she managed to bleat out as she pressed her face hard against the window. There waiting for them was the greatest passenger liner in the world. Some had called it 'The Ship of Dreams'. 'Is…that…the…*Titanic?*' Nana asked again with a great sense of wonder in her voice.

Her father smiled and answering with a chuckle said, 'I cannot see too many other big ships around here, so I guess it probably is.'

The train came to a halt with a bump and in no time passengers were bustling onto the platform alongside the dock where the great ship was berthed.

Nana's father lifted both Mrs Smithers' beautiful leather case and their own luggage down from the shelf above them.

Mrs Smithers thanked Mr Harper as he handed her case to her. 'I do appreciate your help. Thankfully my six trunks are in the baggage car, but this has my jewellery inside so I didn't want to let it out of my sight.'

'Will we be seeing you again on the ship?' Nana enquired expectantly.

'Oh, I don't think so,' Mrs Smithers answered rather pointedly. 'You see I'm travelling first class and you will be second class. Passengers from the different classes are never allowed to mix on board a ship.' She paused before adding, 'Thank you again for helping me. Maybe I will think about the things you have told me sometime. However, I don't think I need to worry about anything terrible happening to me on this ship. Mr Harper, as you very well know the *Titanic* is said to be totally unsinkable!'

Welcome Aboard

Eventually both father and daughter were able to make their way out of their compartment and carefully down onto the platform. There were still many people disembarking from the train. Others were busily trying to collect extra baggage which had been placed, like Mrs Smithers' trunks, in the luggage car at the rear of the carriages.

The platform quickly filled up and was soon crowded with hundreds of excited people all pushing and shoving as they sought to move out of the station towards the great ship. As they too headed for the main exit, Nana caught sight of Mrs Smithers giving instructions to a porter who was struggling with what appeared to be rather a large mountain of trunks.

'Look, Daddy,' she called, pulling at her father's coat sleeve. 'There's the lady we were on the train with. She has got that man to put all her huge cases on to his trolley.'

The two stood and watched as the porter, under the watchful eye of Mrs Smithers, finished loading the cases and began pulling the trolley behind him out of the station, towards the dock side.

'Come on,' her father scolded her with a twinkle in his eye. 'We have to carry our cases to the ship and we don't want to be late and miss it!'

Just as they started off, a small dishevelled boy, with an untidy mop of brown hair, ran towards Nana. He turned to face her and sticking out his tongue and placing his thumbs in his ears, made a funny donkey noise.

Nana recoiled from the dirty-faced boy who seeing the disapproval on her face, said with a strong Liverpool accent, 'I'm sorry, miss, I was dared to do it by me dad.' Then turning quickly in the direction from which he had come he scampered off and was lost in the crowd.

'How strange,' Mr Harper commented as he gazed down at his daughter.

'What did he do that for, Daddy?'

'A dare!'

'What's a dare?'

'Usually a lot of nonsense when someone tries to get someone else to do something stupid for a laugh,' her father answered with a chuckle. 'Maybe the young fellow likes you and was trying to impress you,' he teased.

'I certainly didn't like him,' Nana retorted.

The walk from the station to the *Titanic*, which was docked in berth forty-four, was quite short. However, from the train terminus the passengers were directed out through a small archway and towards a little office. Here a lengthy queue was forming whilst the people were waiting to have their tickets checked.

'Isn't it big!' the little girl exclaimed as she and her father stopped and gazed in admiration at the ship over the top of the dock side buildings. It had gleaming white sides, magnificent yellow-orange funnels tipped with black, and a huge towering mast. These features along with its imposing size gave it a very impressive appearance.

'It certainly is some size of ship,' Mr Harper said to his daughter, as he put their cases down and mopped his brow with a white handkerchief. It was a warm morning and although there was a strong breeze blowing it had not been easy carrying the two heavy suitcases.

'Are you alright, Daddy?' little Nana asked as she turned her concerned countenance towards her father. She often asked her father if he was 'alright'. Nana had become aware that her father did not possess the physical strength that some of her friends' fathers did. She had seen him on many occasions arrive home after an afternoon of visiting sick people and going almost immediately to sleep in his favourite study chair. Although she was only six, the little girl was worried. She worried that perhaps her father may have the awful illness that had taken her mother from her, whilst she was still a baby. She did not want to be an orphan without a mother or a father.

'It's not far now,' Mr Harper sighed, sounding strangely tired. 'Just round this corner,' he smiled as he picked up the two suitcases once again.

'Oh, Daddy, please, let me carry one,' Nana asked eagerly.

'Why, my dear, you would never be able to lift it,' he replied. He placed a suitcase on the ground again and said, 'Here try.'

Taking hold of one of the cases Nana discovered that it came almost up to her chest. She tried to lift it off the ground.

'Oh, Daddy, I can't lift it,' she said with great disappointment.

'Of course you can't,' her father explained. 'It's much too heavy for you. Now, make sure you keep close to me as we join these queues to have our tickets checked.' He paused before picking up the second case and then started forward towards the large white fronted building with a big flag flying above. The flag was coloured red and had a white star in its centre. Across the front of the building written in large black letters were the words 'White Star Line'.

'Why did we have to walk round here, Daddy?' Nana asked almost impatiently. 'Why couldn't we have just walked straight over from the train onto the ship?'

'They need to check our tickets. So it's much easier to do it all at one point here, rather than having everyone rushing forward trying to get onto the boat all at the same time,' her father explained patiently.

Once they were outside the white building they joined one of the long queues of people waiting on the pavement. Mr Harper put the cases down and Nana took hold of his hand.

'Third class this way,' someone shouted. 'Quickly, please,' he called again. As the voice died away, many people started moving out of the queue and in the direction from which the voice had come. The rush of eager people as they pushed past, caused Nana to let go of her father's hand. Soon she was being swept along the pavement by the crowd of moving people.

'Nana!' John Harper called earnestly, as he felt her little hand slip out of his grasp, 'Nana!'

The little girl eventually lost her balance and fell with a thud to the ground.

'Watch the little girl!' cried someone standing in the queue. Nana had fallen at the feet of a kindly-looking middle-aged gentleman and his wife. The gentleman quickly bent down and lifted her to safety.

'Nana!' the call came again.

'Here I am, Daddy,' she called out, as her father came rushing to her aid. 'Here I am. I'm not hurt. At least, not too much.' She answered, trying to rub her head and knee at the same time. 'I got carried away by all those running people,' she explained simply.

'Thankfully she fell onto our feet,' explained the lady. 'But if she had fallen out into the rush she might have been trampled to death. She was very lucky.'

'Thank you so much for your help,' Mr Harper replied. 'But it wasn't luck that saved her. It was the good Lord up in heaven looking after her.'

The couple looked at both father and daughter in a slightly bemused manner and the gentleman replied, 'We are certainly delighted to have been of use to both your daughter and the good Lord.'

Mr Harper shook both their hands in appreciation. Then anxiously looked back down the queue and said, 'We must get back to our suitcases before someone else takes off with them.'

'Why don't you fetch them and come and stand with us?' the lady suggested kindly.

'No, I'm not sure that would be the right thing to do,' Mr Harper replied. 'But thank you both for helping Nana.'

'Maybe we'll see you on board then,' the man said ushering them off with a smile.

Father and daughter walked back the few yards to their belongings. Already some people had stepped over their luggage knocking it to the ground. Mr Harper bent down to retrieve the suitcases before rejoining the rapidly advancing line of passengers.

'Tickets, please. Have your tickets ready, please,' a voice called, as they neared the white fronted building. Towards the apex of the roof Nana noticed that another red flag with a white star had been painted onto the brickwork in a manner that made it look like it was blowing in the breeze.

'What are you looking for?' Nana asked as she observed her father searching through his coat pockets.

'These,' he answered pulling out a pair of tickets with a flourish and waving them in front of his little daughter. 'Our tickets! We must have them ready for the man to see. Look, we have ticket number 248727.' He bent down and showed the tickets to his daughter.

'How much was it?' she asked curiously.

'Very expensive,' her father replied and then bending down to her he whispered into her ear, 'Promise you will not tell anyone?' The little girl nodded with a smile. 'They cost thirty-three pounds!'

'Daddy!' Nana exclaimed. 'That is a lot of money. I think that is more than I have ever seen in all my life.'

'I think it is more than I have seen too,' her father laughed back at her.

Soon they found themselves standing in front of a rather authoritative-looking man, wearing a blue and white cap. He also sported the white star badge in the lapel of his jacket. Taking the tickets he scrutinised them thoroughly, before allowing them both through the gate and onto the berth where the ship lay.

Nana and her father gazed again in amazement at the sheer scale of the ship, now that they were standing almost alongside it. Everything was big. Very big! Nana looked up at the clean, white, sparkling upper reaches of the ship. She noted the various open decks with people moving along them, going to and fro in a flurry of activity. She saw the huge stern with its smooth curves that disappeared down at a crazy angle towards the sea. She wondered why, with such

27

a massive overhang, the top did not break off and tumble into the water. Her father, also looking up, was impressed by the four giant funnels, and the two huge masts rising from the ship's decks. It really did appear to be a ship beyond anybody's dreams!

'Come on, come on!' someone rudely said, as they tried to push past father and daughter. 'Get a move on! What are you staring at? Have you never seen a ship before? Get out of the way!'

'We'd better move on,' Mr Harper said to his daughter as he gave her a friendly push. 'Keep tight hold of my coat sleeve,' he cautioned as they made their way towards the ramps, that extended from the quayside onto the great ocean liner. 'We don't want you to be trampled on again do we?'

As they progressed Mr Harper saw a ramp near the stern with a notice saying 'Second Class Passengers', hanging above the gangway. 'This must be the way,' he said, and the two of them turned and started making their way up the ramp that led into the side of the ship. As they reached the top there was another sign which said 'C Deck'.

'Your tickets, please,' someone in a uniform asked rather coldly as they stepped onto the deck. Nana's father fumbled in his pockets once again and producing the required tickets, handed them to the man.

The steward looked at them carefully before saying, 'Room D87.' He then turned to the plan of the ship that he was holding in his hand and mumbled over to himself, 'Room D87,' as he searched for its position on his plan. 'Ah, here it is,' he said with a note of triumph in his voice. 'Sorry about that, but with it being a new ship none of us quite know where everything is yet. Anyway, you need to go down the main staircase to the second class dining saloon on Deck D. Turn right and right again into the corridor then it's at the bottom of the third corridor on your left on the starboard side.'

'Thank you,' said Mr Harper as he once again picked up the two cases.

'That sounds rather complicated,' Nana said looking at her father. 'Do you think we will remember it all?'

'We shall try,' her father replied, and added, 'Come on, Nana, your adventure is just about to begin!'

Exploration Time

As they walked down the stairs they were met by several passengers coming up. Each of them was complaining.

'We can't find our rooms,' one said.

'It's hopeless!' another added.

'There's no one to help down here at all! Total chaos!' a third grumbled as he searched for a steward to vent his frustration on.

Father and daughter continued on their way down the oak staircase with its red carpet. After one flight of stairs they came to a room marked 'Dining Saloon'.

'We're almost there, Nana. All we have to do is turn right here and right again.' John Harper led his daughter past a pair of glass-panelled swing doors that led into the dining area then, turning right, they found the rather narrow corridor that led to their cabin.

'You count with me,' Nana's father suggested. 'We have to count three passageways on the left. Will you help me?'

The little girl looked up and said, 'Oh, yes,' as they passed by the first opening. 'One,' she said out loud, 'two, three. Daddy, this is it!'

'I sincerely hope so,' her father replied as they turned down an even narrower passageway. Nana ran on ahead to the end of the short corridor and shouted, 'Here we are.'

Her father came up behind, laden down with the burden of his two suitcases. 'Yes, D87,' he responded. 'This is our cabin.' He placed the cases on the ground, opened the door and allowed his daughter to lead the way inside.

The door opened into a room with bunk beds at one end and a small porthole on the other. On the far wall was a tall elegant writing bureau with drawers beneath. Next to this was a wardrobe with double opening doors that ran almost from ceiling height to the floor. The carpet was a plush green and Nana felt her shoes sink into its thick soft covering. Placed underneath the porthole was a settee, covered in a rich gold fabric, that made it look, to Nana's eyes, as though it belonged in some grand castle or palace. The little girl ran with delight to look out of the porthole. She stood on her tiptoes, but still couldn't see out. She looked pleadingly at her father.

'Please, may I climb on to the sofa to look out, Daddy?' she enquired hopefully.

'Of course you may,' he replied happily. 'Just so long as you take your shoes off first.'

The little girl kicked off her little leather shoes and climbed with glee up onto the sofa. Even standing on that, she had to take hold of the brass surround of the window and pull herself up onto her tiptoes in order to see out.

'Oh, there are some birds out there,' she said as she gazed across the sea towards the far side of the docking area, where one or two smaller ships were berthed.

'Yes,' her father replied, happy that his daughter was so excited. 'They will be seagulls, possibly herring gulls or maybe black-headed gulls just coming out of their winter plumage.'

'When can we go and explore, Daddy?'

'In a minute. Let's get the suitcases sorted first. We will, after all, be on this ship for quite a long time.'

It took her father about ten minutes to unpack their luggage. Nana kept herself occupied watching the seagulls circling and diving alongside the ship. Once he had finished sorting out their clothes, Mr Harper stowed the suitcases underneath the bottom bunk bed and turning to his daughter said, 'Let's take a look around this amazing ship.'

The two left the cabin and retracing their steps through the narrow corridors, made their way back towards the second class dining saloon. On entering it, they were impressed by the size and luxury of the room. It was huge, extending the whole breadth of the ship, with space to seat around four hundred people. Large marble pillars were positioned every so often along the full length of the room, giving it a majestic appearance. The chairs were made of wood with ornate legs and beautiful red leather seats and backs. The silver cutlery was already laid on the table and beside each place setting was a starched white napkin, folded like a small party hat. Nana rubbed her feet along the thick carpet pile, which had a rather striking mural pattern in a deep maroon colour. It was Nana who spoke first. 'Daddy, it is so beautiful.'

Her father looked at her and answered thoughtfully, 'Yes, it is beautiful.'

'Do you think heaven will be as nice as this?' the little girl quizzed her father.

'I am very certain that heaven will be much grander and finer than even the wonderful rooms that those travelling first class will be enjoying,' he answered.

'So will Mummy be in a better place than we are?' Nana continued.

'My dear,' her father replied as he squatted down beside her, 'there is nothing here to compare to the wonderful things to be found in heaven. Why, heaven is heaven because the Lord Jesus is there and he fills it with his glory and beauty and nothing here on earth can compare with that. The Bible says, "Eye hath not seen, nor ear heard, neither have entered into the heart of man, the things that God hath prepared for those that love Him".'

'Oh, Daddy,' the little girl said earnestly, 'won't it be wonderful to meet Mummy there with the Lord Jesus and for us all to be together in that lovely place.'

'It certainly will! It most certainly will!' her father replied, longing to see his Saviour and his wife again.

'So we meet again,' a familiar voice said, as they made their way out of the dining saloon and towards the main staircase. Nana looked round to see the man at whose feet she had been thrown in the crush, a couple of hours earlier. 'Wonderful ship, isn't it?' he remarked, as his wife walked up the stairs to join him.

'Yes, I overheard one of the stewards quoting the papers which said, "It was a magnificent symbol of man's greatest achievements, finally overcoming all the elements that nature can throw at it". So I suppose,' the gentleman said, adding with a chuckle, 'we will be safer here on this ship than we ever would be back home.'

Nana, who was busy looking at the wonderful array of pictures and books that adorned the walls of the second class library, suddenly spoke up.

'My daddy often says that the only really safe thing to trust in is the Lord Jesus, isn't that so, Daddy?'

'Yes, my dear, that is very true,' her father answered adding. 'It is better to trust in the Lord than to put confidence in man.' The couple stood open-mouthed at both father and daughter before the lady answered, 'So you really meant what you said earlier about God protecting your daughter.'

'Yes, I prayed especially today that God would keep her safe on this journey and the Lord used you to answer that prayer,' Mr Harper replied.

The lady looked at the little girl, who by now was growing a bit restless and bouncing up and down, tugging at her father's sleeve. 'Come on, Daddy, I am sure there is so much to see.'

'Yes, you must show your daughter the ship for it really is quite something, but perhaps you would like to join us here for dinner tonight,' she enquired, looking thoughtfully into the preacher's face.

'Yes, we'd be delighted, wouldn't we, Nana?' he replied.

'Only if we can look round the boat first, Daddy,' his daughter's shrill voice answered back, causing them all to laugh heartily.

'We'll meet you here at 7 p.m. for dinner,' the man said. 'I must tell you our names, I am Earnest Collings and this is my wife Lillian.'

'Delighted to meet you,' Nana's father replied courteously. 'I am John Harper and this is my daughter, Annie Jessie, but I call her Nana. So seven it is then. We will look forward to your company.'

With that, Nana pulled her father away saying, 'I want to go outside, Daddy. Let's go.'

The two passed into the library through glass-panelled double doors following a sign that said 'Elevator'. Once through the doors they found another wooden staircase that led in both directions from the deck they were on. A notice was hanging above the stairway, pointing up, which said, 'Smoke Room, Promenade Deck' and another notice pointing down saying, 'Dining Saloon, Cabins'. In the middle of the stairway was the elevator shaft with its sliding metal gate that looked to Nana like a wild animal's cage.

'Let's try this,' her father suggested, as he pushed a small button situated on the right hand side of the gate.

'What is it, Daddy?' Nana asked inquisitively.

'It's an elevator, my dear. It will take us to the deck without having to walk up all the stairs.'

'Wow! I've never been in one of those before,' Nana replied excitedly.

'I haven't been in one too often either,' her father answered with a chuckle. 'So I guess it will be a real treat for both of us.'

The elevator whirred down its shaft and came to a halt behind the metal gate and Nana could see that a second metal gate fronted the lift itself. A young man wearing a royal blue uniform with double breasted jacket, fastened with gold buttons and a matching hat, opened the gates in order to allow the two into the elevator.

'Where to, sir?' he enquired courteously.

'The Promenade deck, please,' Mr Harper replied.

The young man closed both gates and pressed a button on the bank of switches. The elevator started with a bump that made Nana jump with surprise. Up it went, the excited little girl squeaking with delight as it slowly passed various levels, each with signs that could be read through the gates. 'Deck B – 2nd Class Smoke Room', 'Deck A – First Class Smoke Room' and finally 'Boat Deck – 2nd Class Promenade'. The lift came to a halt and the young man opened the two gates saying, 'Second Class Promenade Deck, sir.'

'Thank you,' said Nana's father as they stepped out and felt the breeze as it blew around the ship. Just then a whistle called shrilly and several people moved over to the port side where they were able to see the arrival of the second boat train from London, this time carrying the first class passengers. Nana and her father struggled to see what was happening as the lifeboats hanging in their davits blocked their view along that part of the deck. Eventually they managed to get into a position between the lifeboats where they could see the first class passengers disembark from the train. They watched as carriage doors opened and men and women climbed out dressed in every sort of finery you could imagine. Ladies wore full flowing dresses, exquisite bonnets and carried fancy parasols. The men were in fine suits with tall top hats and white gloves that seemed to be carried more as an accessory than for any real use. Nana and her father saw an array of different shaped and sized trunks being unloaded from the boat train and pulled by cart across to the ship. Suddenly a man's voice called out from the watching crowd on the boat deck. 'Look! There's Mr Strauss and his wife.' All eyes turned to where the man was pointing.

'Who's Mr Strauss?' enquired Nana.

'He's a very wealthy man,' her father answered simply. 'He owns a big department store in New York.'

'Daddy, I don't think I can see him. Please, will you lift me up so I can?'

Her father bent down and lifted her up so that she was able see better over the side of the boat.

'Which one is he?' she asked.

'That one there with the beard and tall hat,' her father replied, pointing towards an elderly-looking man who was walking towards the ramp leading up into the front of the ship.

'Who's that with him?'

'His wife, I guess.'

The little girl looked at the elderly lady on Mr Strauss' arm who was wearing a voluminous brown dress with matching hat, sporting ornate ostrich plumes. She appeared to be busy chatting to the porters carrying her personal luggage on to the boat.

'Do you think we will get to meet them?' Nana enquired.

'Oh, I don't think so,' replied Mr Harper. 'They're in first class and we're in second. It's a pity though, as I'd love to tell them about God's Son. Well, who knows, the Lord can do wonderful things. He may yet provide a way for me to tell that gentleman and his wife about heaven? You just never know!'

A Near Miss

The air was suddenly filled with a deafening noise. Nana jumped with surprise and instinctively covered her ears with her hands. The frightening noise had come from the two forward funnels of the ship. Nana looked in that direction, still with her hands to her ears. She saw little wisps of steam puffing from the giant whistles that sat proudly on the huge funnels. The sound stopped and Nana relaxed and let her hands drop, only to quickly raise them to her ears again as another deep roar came from the funnels and reverberated around the docks. She thought it must have been heard in New York. It was so loud! Another pause and then a third loud boom echoed into the midday air and finally died away. As quietness filled the air again, cautiously she let her hands drop once more from her ears.

'What was that noise, Daddy?' she asked, looking rather shaken.

'That,' her father answered, 'was the traditional three hoots that a ship gives when it's ready to leave the port.'

'Oh, but why does it have to be so loud and frightening?'

Her father smiled, 'I guess that the biggest ship in the world just has to be the loudest ship in the world!

Let's go and watch the tugs move us out of the berth.'

'You'll get a better view from down on the promenade of B Deck,' said a middle-aged man dressed in a white star uniform. 'You can't see much from up here with the lifeboats, and the forward part of this deck is reserved for the posh folk in first class. Go down to B Deck and you'll see much better.'

'Thank you very much,' Mr Harper replied. 'We'll do that.'

'Can we take the lift again, Daddy?' Nana enquired hopefully.

'Not this time. I think it may be quicker if we used the stairs. Come on, I'll race you down!'

Once on the promenade of B Deck they realised that what the man had said was true. They did indeed have a much better view over the side of the ship.

For a short while they watched the seemingly tiny tug boats pulling, pushing and manoeuvring the great ship away from Berth 44 and out towards the open river. Once in the river, the tugs turned the ship to point out towards the open sea. Then she started up her own engines and her three giant propellers began to revolve slowly and take them down the river.

Mr Harper was just about to suggest to Nana that they head back to their cabin when they heard a noise and clamour from the other side of the deck. Indistinct voices were shouting at one another, people started moving over towards the port side of the ship.

'Come on, Nana, let's see what's going on,' her father said. He took her hand and joined the others who were heading round to the other side of the ship.

'There'll be a collision!' they heard someone call out. 'Look that ship's drifting straight for us!'

'It's snapped its mooring lines,' another yelled.

'It's the draught from the *Titanic*, it's broken that other ship's cables and it's now pulling it towards us,' an alarmed voice tried to explain.

Staring out, Nana and her father could see that a large ship was loose in the water and drifting straight for the *Titanic*. Everyone felt their ship slow down as the engines were put into reverse, but still the stern of the other ship drifted ominously closer to the side of their vessel. They watched spellbound as a tug moved rapidly round to the far side of the drifting ship and men on the tug threw a line onto the loose vessel. Within seconds it was made secure and the tug started to take up the strain in the hope of pulling the boat clear of the *Titanic's* side. Nana felt the other ship had come so close she would be able to jump across the gap between the two. Then slowly, ever so slowly, she saw the other ship begin to move away as the line secured to the tug boat held firm, pulling the drifting ship safely out of danger.

'Wow!' someone called. 'That was a close one.'

'What happened, Daddy?' Nana asked her father, not having understood what she had heard or seen.

'I think that what happened is that the waves made by the *Titanic* caused that other ship to break the ropes that were holding it to the dock side and caused her to drift towards us. So we had to stop so that it didn't hit us,' he explained, as simply as he could.

There was a delay as the *Titanic* waited in the middle of the river, whilst the tugs pulled the other ship to safety. The *New York,* as everyone now knew it to be called, was pulled in front of the *Titanic* down the river and towed around a small headland and into the safety of another dock. Then there was a further wait as a ship called *Oceanic*, that some on the dock side feared may too be in danger of breaking its mooring cables as the *Titanic* passed, had extra lines attached to hold it safely in position.

It was an hour later before the ship started up her engines again. As she reached the river mouth she stopped to allow the port pilot and unwanted crew to disembark. Then she gracefully sailed out to sea and on her way towards Cherbourg in France.

After all the excitement of the day, little Nana was feeling very tired and wanted to go back to the cabin. Her father, too, was glad of a chance to rest and an opportunity to read his Bible. He had taken several Bibles with him including a large leather volume he used for preaching and a small New Testament that had been given to him by his wife on their wedding day. However, it was another copy that he had in his hands as settled into a chair beside Nana's bunk. Usually, he rose early in the morning to pray and read God's Word, but there had been so much to do this morning in preparation for their journey that he had only time for a short prayer to ask God for help and guidance for their day. As Nana dozed in the bunk below him, her father took out his well worn leather-bound Bible and began to finger the pages that he loved and knew so well. His eyes fell on a verse that he had often read, 'It is a good thing to give thanks unto the Lord'.

'Yes,' he thought, 'I have much to be thankful for: a wonderful Saviour, a lovely daughter, a lot of fine Christian friends. The Lord has certainly taken care of us so far today!' He climbed down from his bunk and fell upon his knees next to the sofa and began to pray.

'Daddy,' a little voice piped up about an hour later, 'Daddy, I'm hungry.'

Her father slowly and rather stiffly lifted himself up from where he had been praying and turned towards his daughter who was still lying on her bed. 'Yes, I think I am too,' he answered cheerfully. 'It has been a long and rather eventful day so far.'

'A lot has certainly happened,' his daughter agreed, pulling back the bedcover as she lifted herself out of the bunk. 'It's been so exciting and I am glad to be coming with you.'

'I'm glad you are too, my dear,' he answered, bending down and giving his daughter a hug, 'I really am.' He paused before standing upright and saying, 'It's almost time to meet up with Mr and Mrs Collings in the dining saloon. Let's get washed and changed.'

A steward, dressed in a gleaming white jacket and black trousers, greeted them as they entered into the dining saloon.

'Good evening, sir,' he said to Nana's father. 'Will you be dining tonight?'

'Yes, please,' her father responded, in his Scottish accent. 'We have plans to meet up with a Mr and Mrs Collings.'

'Ah, yes, sir,' the steward answered, as a look of recognition crossed his face. 'They have just arrived themselves and are over here. Follow me.'

The steward led them across the dining room to where Mr Collings and his wife were sitting. 'Your friends, sir,' he said, as he pulled chairs out from under the table in order to allow both Nana and her father to sit down.

'Ah!' said the gentleman in recognition. 'So good to see you both again.' Then taking a special interest in Nana, he added, 'It's especially nice to see this delightful young lady who fell at my feet earlier today!'

Nana smiled a little shyly as she recalled the unpleasant incident of being pulled away from her father by the rushing crowd.

'Now, what are we all going to eat this evening?' Mr Collings said jovially as he passed round the menus that were on the table. He excused himself as he sneezed into a white handkerchief he had pulled from his trouser pocket. 'I seem to be suffering from a touch of the cold.'

'Oh, not to worry,' Mr Harper answered, 'I guess it's the result of the good old British weather.'

The food was ordered, and soon brought by two waitresses in full length black dresses with small white aprons. Once they had all received their meal, each looked at the other slightly uneasily. It was Nana's father who spoke first. 'I hope that you won't mind if we give thanks to God for this meal.'

Mr and Mrs Collings looked from one to another and then across at the Harpers. 'Lillian and I were just about to say the same to you. You see we are Christians too.'

'Praise the Lord,' Nana's father exclaimed. 'Let's thank the Lord together.' And with that, all four bowed their heads as they gave thanks to the Lord for the food that had been provided.

As they tucked into their meal, Mr Collings asked Mr Harper, 'Would you be a church minister?'

'Yes, I am a Baptist minister at Walworth Road Baptist Church in London, but I was born in Scotland. Where do you both come from?'

'London, as well,' Mr Collings replied. 'I am vicar of St Jude's Church in Whitechapel.'

'If I'm right, is that not a rather run down area of London?'

'Yes, that's so. There are people living in that area with many difficult backgrounds, but each has the same need of the Lord Jesus Christ as Saviour.'

'Absolutely true,' replied Nana's father. 'It's the basic need of every person in the world.'

Mrs Collings left the men to their conversation and turned to Nana. 'Have you left your mother behind or are you travelling to meet her?'

'Oh, I'll meet her one day,' Nana answered, 'when I get to heaven.'

'Oh, I didn't realise. I am sorry, my dear. I really am,' Mrs Collings replied, blushing slightly.

'She died when I was born, but I have her picture here in my locket if you'd like to see?' Nana continued.

'Oh, yes please,' the lady said, lifting the pair of spectacles that hung around her neck to her eyes, in order to take a proper look. She moved her chair closer as Nana lifted the silver locket, unclipped the clasp to reveal the photograph. 'You certainly have your mother's fine looks,' the lady beamed across at her.

'She has those alright,' Mr Harper said, with a smile, joining in their conversation.

'You know,' said Mr Collings, 'we thought you must be a Christian when you corrected my wife after she had said that Nana had been lucky.'

'Oh, dear,' Mr Harper said with a wry smile, 'I hope I did not come across like a schoolteacher, correcting you?'

'Not at all,' Mrs Collings replied. 'Earnest here, is often telling me that I should not speak about luck. I know as a Christian there is no such thing. Our lives are in the Lord's hands and we know that he does all things well.'

'I also was thinking of our conversation earlier about the greatness of this ship,' Mr Collings confessed. 'You are right, it is no use placing confidence in man's ability to create something as beautiful and indestructible as this ship. Like you, I do believe that it is only when we place our confidence in the Lord, that we are really safe. If we boast too much about the ability of this ship's designers and builders, then God may just show us how small we are and how great he is!'

'Perhaps that is what this world needs in order to appreciate God's way of salvation!' Mrs Collings added.

The Richest Man

They were still eating their meal as they arrived outside the French port of Cherbourg. Mr Collings and Mr Harper continued to chat away whilst Mrs Collings and Nana watched some people who were milling around outside the dining saloon. Mrs Collings said to Nana, 'I think they must be trying to catch a glimpse of the ferry boats transporting the new passengers to our ship.' Two boats named *Nomadic* and *Traffic* had been specially built to carry the passengers out to the *Titanic* and her sister ship, *Olympic*.

They could hear some voices speaking in French and Nana was eager to go outside to see what was happening. Having finished their meals, Mrs Collings excused Nana and herself and took the little girl out on to the deck so that she could see France or at least the harbour town of Cherbourg.

Mr Harper and Mr Collings soon joined them and although it was beginning to get dark they were still able to look out and see the circular designed sea walls that protected the harbour and the distant lights of the town itself. The large ferry, *Nomadic,* had its own impressive size dwarfed, as it anchored alongside the iron hull of the *Titanic*. They all watched as the new passengers continued to disembark from the *Nomadic* through an open door halfway down the side of the ship.

Mr and Mrs Collings carried on watching for a few more minutes and then, declaring that they were feeling rather tired, they bade Nana and her father goodnight. Mr Collings added, 'We will see you in the morning, Nana, and you too Mr Harper, sleep well.'

'Goodnight Mr and Mrs Collings,' Nana said yawning herself.

'Yes, goodnight. It was lovely to have spent the evening with you,' Mr Harper added. Then turning to Nana he said, 'My dear, ten more minutes then I think we too should retire to our cabin.'

'Alright, Daddy,' Nana replied rather quietly.

'Look,' her father suddenly exclaimed, 'There's Mr Astor with his new wife.'

Nana looked, as a tall elegant man in his forties climbed carefully from the smaller ship onto the *Titanic*, before turning round in order to offer his hand to help his wife across.

'Who's Mr Astor?' Nana enquired.

'Some say he's the richest man in the world,' Mr Harper replied.

'Richer than Mr and Mrs Strauss?' Nana asked excitedly.

'Most possibly,' he answered. 'He's just married again and his new wife is very young.'

'And very pretty,' his daughter remarked, looking at the young lady, who by now had crossed from one boat to the other and was disappearing into the body of the great ship.

'They have been in France for a few weeks, to try and escape some bad publicity.' Mr Harper didn't mention it to Nana but Mr Astor had gone through a nasty divorce and the press were pestering him and his new wife. 'I would love to be able to speak to Mr Astor as well as Mr Strauss about heavenly wealth,' Nana's father continued.

'Ner, ner, de, ner, ner,' a cheeky voice piped up, as Nana felt a hand tap her on her left shoulder. She swung round just in time to see a boy with a grin on his face disappearing quickly along the deck of the ship.

'Daddy,' she declared, 'that's the same boy who stuck his tongue out at me on the station this morning.'

'So it is,' her father answered. 'Twice in a day! I think maybe he really does like you!'

'Oh, Daddy, stop teasing,' Nana replied, with a giggle as she turned to look alongside the ship once again.

After a few more minutes, they heard the great iron door in the side of the *Titanic* pulled closed with a thud. The smaller craft chugged slowly back towards the port of Cherbourg.

'That's your ten minutes up, so it's time for bed, I think,' Mr Harper declared, as they watched the last rays of sun sinking down beyond the horizon.

They had just arrived back in their cabin when they felt the ship's engines start up and knew that they were once more on their way, this time to Queenstown on the southern tip of Ireland. Nana's father helped her into her nightdress before kneeling at the side of her bunk and asking her, as he always did, if there was anything that she wanted him to pray about.

'Not really, Daddy,' came the reply from a tired girl, but then after some thought she said, 'but I would like to have a friend near to my own age to play with.'

'Very well,' her father replied, 'we shall pray about that then.' He held his daughter's hand and closed his eyes, thanking God for his Son, for safety, for the ship they were on and asking that his daughter might find a friend. Once he had finished, he pulled out his little pocket New Testament, that he always carried, and read a few verses from it. As he finished, he turned to kiss his daughter goodnight and smiled to himself as he discovered that she was already asleep.

The next morning dawned clear and bright as Mr Harper dropped quietly down from his bunk at his usual rising time of 5.30 a.m. He headed to the bathroom which was located just next door. Once washed and clothed he again knelt in silent prayer and spent time reading his Bible. Every now and then he glanced across at his daughter who was still sleeping soundly. As the little girl opened her eyes she sleepily asked, 'Daddy where are we?'

'We are on the *Titanic* travelling to America,' he replied.

The little girl opened her eyes wider and answered, 'Oh, yes, I remember. We are on the ship of dreams!'

Friends and Foes

As usual Mr Harper slipped his little New Testament into his pocket before taking Nana down to the dining saloon for breakfast. Whilst eating some warm toast, Nana caught sight of several children and in particular a little girl who was carrying a very large and cuddly teddy bear. 'Oh, Daddy!' Nana exclaimed, 'look at the beautiful teddy that girl is holding!'

The other girl's father, on hearing Nana's comment, stopped as he passed by the table and turned to speak to his daughter.

'Eva, let the little girl have a hold of your teddy bear.'

'No!' the little girl answered back determinedly, 'I won't. It's my teddy bear.'

Gently the father coaxed his young daughter. 'I know it's your teddy bear, but it would be kind to just let this little girl hold it for a while.'

Rather reluctantly, the child handed the teddy bear over to Nana who took it and gave its silky soft fur a loving stroke.

'That's very kind of you,' Mr Harper said to the girl who was standing watching. 'Does it have a name?'

The little girl remained silent. Her eyes fixed upon Nana still holding her bear.

'No,' her father chuckled, 'We just call it teddy.'

'I think it's a beautiful bear,' Mr Harper continued, 'and I think Nana does too, don't you, my dear?'

'Oh, yes, Daddy, it's a lovely, sweet bear and I wish I had one just like it.'

Both fathers laughed and Mr Harper answered, 'Maybe when we reach Chicago, if you are really good, we'll see if we can get one for you.'

'Oh, will you, Daddy, will you?' Nana begged, suddenly loosing interest in the bear she was holding. 'I have always wanted a teddy bear. I really have!'

'We'll just have to see,' Mr Harper replied, with a twinkle in his eye. 'Now, I think you had better give this teddy back to its owner.'

Gently giving the teddy a last hug, Nana handed the precious bear back to the other girl and thanked her.

'My name is Benjamin Harrison,' the man offered, looking at Nana's father, 'and this is my daughter, Eva and just over there is my wife, Esther.'

'Pleased to meet you,' Nana's father replied. 'I'm John Harper and this is my daughter, Nana.'

'And my mummy isn't here, because she is in heaven,' Nana added, before anyone had a chance to enquire about her mother.

'Oh, dear,' the man said, looking compassionately at Nana, 'I am sorry to hear that.'

'There's no need to be sorry, Mr Harrison,' replied Nana easily. 'She's in a much better place, you know.'

There was a short silence before Mr Harper spoke up and explained, 'My wife died shortly after Nana was born.'

'Oh, I see,' the man said, still amazed at Nana's bluntness. 'Maybe the two girls could meet some time and play together.'

'Yes, that would be really lovely, wouldn't it, Nana?' Mr Harper replied, turning to his daughter. 'I'm sure the two of them will get along just fine.'

Later that morning, the girls joined up just outside the dining saloon where they amused themselves together for a couple of hours, leaving their parents free to chat and drink coffee. As the two girls played excitedly, the cheeky-faced boy suddenly reappeared round the corner of the main staircase. Nana recognised the face instantly and scowling said, 'Oh, it's you again!'

The boy stood staring at the two girls for a while before saying, 'Hello, I'm Charlie Applewhite. What are your names?'

'My daddy does not like me talking to naughty boys,' Nana answered somewhat haughtily.

'Aw, I've only been 'aving a bit of fun,' the boy answered meekly, clearly taken aback by Nana's curtness.

'Who is he?' Eva asked Nana, glancing at the boy, but not daring to meet his gaze.

'I don't know, but I first met him yesterday at the station when he stuck his tongue out at me. Then later on when we were on the ship, he tapped me on the back and ran off,' answered Nana in a rather cross tone.

'Oh,' replied Eva mischievously and rather loudly, 'my daddy says boys that do those sort of things to you, usually like you.'

'Ugh!' Charlie replied, 'Girls! Who wants to like girls? I'm off,' and with that he turned and dashed up the stairs and out of sight.

'Well, that got rid of him,' said Eva, a note of triumph in her voice.

'Let's carry on with our game,' replied Nana, relieved that the boy had disappeared.

It was lunch time and the *Titanic* was anchored just outside the port of Queenstown in Southern Ireland. She was waiting to collect more passengers and mail before heading out across the Atlantic Ocean to America.

As they sat eating their lunch, Nana spoke to her father and said, 'It is nice to have a friend, Daddy.'

'It most certainly is,' her father replied. 'A friend is a great thing and it is lovely you seem to have found one in Eva.'

Nana beamed, 'She's such good fun and not at all like she was at breakfast, when she wasn't keen on letting me hold her teddy bear. Why, this morning we have played wooden tops, hoopla, hide and seek as well as several running games up on the Promenade Deck'.

'I am glad that you have been having such a great time,' her father replied, as he tucked into a juicy brown sausage. 'I just hope that you weren't annoying any of the passengers with your shenanigans.'

'What are Sinan…Shenann…'

'You mean shenanigans,' her father laughed. 'It means the naughty things you get up to.'

'Oh, no,' Nana answered with a look of shock on her face. 'Eva and I haven't been getting up to anything naughty at all.'

Her father laughed again, 'I know that. I was only teasing you! But just make sure you don't annoy anyone.'

'I wouldn't want to do that, Daddy,' Nana replied, relieved that he wasn't really thinking she had been naughty.

'Daddy, we did…' her voice trailed away as if she was pondering what to say next, 'we did meet that boy again.'

'What! The one who pulled a face at you,' her father answered, smiling.

'He stuck his tongue out at me,' Nana corrected her father in a serious voice. 'He found us in the dining saloon and said he was called Charlie.'

'That figures,' Mr Harper replied.

'What do you mean?'

'Cheeky Charlie! That's what I'd have called him after his carrying on yesterday,' her father answered.

'Cheeky Charlie. Yes, that suits him.'

Having finished their lunch father and daughter walked out onto the deck to view the tender that had been bringing more passengers to the ship from Queenstown. The little ship came alongside the *Titanic* and was held in position to allow passengers to pass safely across. Nana thought that some of these new passengers looked a bit rough, especially some of the men. Then she saw a couple of ladies being helped up and changed her mind. These ladies were wearing simple, full length dresses. They had few embellishments by way of fine jewellery and ornate hats. She thought they seemed different to the ladies like Mrs Smithers, who had been travelling first class.

'Are those ladies like my mummy was?' she asked, looking up at her father.

'Yes, I suppose they are a bit,' her father answered, rather quietly. He turned away and continued, 'We could go and have a look at the books in the library? If we find a nice story, I'll read it to you if you like.'

'Oh, that would be great,' Nana replied enthusiastically.

As they made their way along the promenade deck to the library, three young men, all looking rather unkempt and dirty, came running up the stairs and pushed past Nana and her father, causing them to almost fall to the floor. The men continued on through a doorway and down another passage, disappearing from view.

'Please, be careful,' Nana's father called after them, as he sought to regain his balance. Then before he'd had time to ask his daughter if she was alright, a steward in a white star uniform ran up the stairs and stopped at the top, puffing and out of breath.

'Did you see three men come up here?' he asked hoarsely.

'Yes,' Nana's father replied. 'They pushed past us and ran through there.' He pointed to the door through which the three had gone.

'Thanks,' the man answered hurriedly, before darting through the door and after them.

'I wonder what that was all about?' Nana's father commented, as he closed the library door behind him.

'They were not nice men, Daddy,' replied Nana.

'Never mind,' he said. 'Let's look at the books.'

In the library, the two of them found a selection of children's books and Nana pulled out a large book of nursery rhymes with big colourful illustrations. She turned the pages over, looking at the various pictures of kings, queens, odd-looking animals and strangely dressed people. 'Daddy,' she said, as she continued turning the pages, 'look at these funny pictures.'

Her father looked down over her shoulder and smiled at the pictures his daughter had discovered. He continued to watch as she picked out another book and again began to turn its pages in her small hands.

'I'll just sit down over there,' her father said, pointing at a leather chair that was placed just underneath a window.

Just as he sat down, the two great steam whistles sounded again and Nana looked across at her father and tried to shout above the noise. 'Does that mean we are now leaving here and going to America?'

'Yes, I guess it does,' he answered. 'Very soon England and Ireland will be way behind us and we will be out into the Atlantic Ocean.'

Lost Testament

'What are you looking for?' Nana asked her father, as she watched him rummaging through his pockets. 'Have you lost something?'

'Yes,' he replied, without stopping his search, 'I can't find my New Testament. I had it when we left the cabin this morning. I don't know what could have happened to it.'

'I bet one of those rough men stole it,' Nana suggested bluntly.

'Don't be silly,' answered her father as he again fumbled with an inside pocket of his jacket. 'They only bumped into me. I'll have to see if I left it in the dining saloon.'

Just as he finished speaking, Eva and her father walked into the library. 'Nana, are you coming to play with me?' Eva asked, as she sat down beside her. 'The boat has just started moving again.'

'Yes, we heard the whistles.' Turning to her father she asked, 'Is it alright if I play with Eva?'

Her father, who was peering underneath the chair he had been sitting on, looked up at Eva's father and said, 'That will be fine, as long as it does not cause you any trouble, Mr Harrison. If you don't mind I must return to the dining saloon.'

'Not at all, Harper,' Eva's father responded jovially. 'The two of them played so well together this morning that I was keen Eva should meet up with Nana again. My wife's doing some writing in our cabin, so I have the child-minding responsibility this afternoon.' As he watched Mr Harper stand up, he asked, 'Have you lost something?'

'Yes, as a matter of fact, I have,' he replied, wearing a worried expression. 'I cannot find my New Testament.'

'It's been stolen,' Nana piped up again.

'Now, Nana dear,' her father scolded her, 'I am sure it hasn't. I think I just left it in the dining saloon when we had lunch,' he paused. Nana's father then added, 'If it's all right I'll leave Nana with you, Mr Harrison, whilst I go and see if I can find it.'

Nana and Eva played happily all afternoon, looking at books and exploring some of the different rooms in second class. Eva's father had searched out some of the more interesting areas of the ship for them to see. When they came up on deck, they found that the faster forward motion of the ship caused a stiff breeze and the two girls enjoyed facing the wind so that it blew through their long hair, making it flow out behind them.

When teatime finally arrived, both families sat together. 'Have you found your missing Bible?' Mr Harrison enquired, in a friendly manner.

'No, I haven't,' Mr Harper replied. 'I know I had it before lunch, but after that it just disappeared into thin air.'

'One of those rough men who bumped into you stole it,' his daughter again told him from across the table.

'Who is she talking about?' Eva's father asked.

'Oh, just three men who pushed past us when we were on our way to the library after lunch,' Mr Harper answered. 'There was a steward chasing them.'

Eva's father leant forward, 'You know, Harper, they might have been steerage passengers and could well have taken your New Testament when they collided with you.'

'I don't think so,' Nana's father responded, with a doubtful look. 'What would they want with my New Testament?'

'I guess they were hoping it was your wallet,' Mr Harrison suggested.

'It's a possibility, I suppose,' Mr Harper answered.

'Was it valuable?' Eva's mother asked, as she entered the conversation.

'Well, it's God's Word, so it is very valuable but what makes it extra special is that it was given to me by my wife on our wedding day. But never mind, I'm sure it will turn up somewhere,' Mr Harper concluded, with a note of hopeful optimism in his voice.

The three adults and the two children tucked into the sumptuous food that was once again placed before them. The adults chatted amiably, whilst the two girls talked and giggled non-stop to one another.

Just as they were finishing a wonderful ice cream dessert, Charlie appeared at the table.

'Hello,' he said brightly to the two girls. 'Have you finished eating?'

'Yes, we have,' Eva answered politely.

'Then do you want to come and play?' he asked, ignoring the gaze of Eva's parents as they were studying his somewhat dishevelled clothing and unkempt appearance.

'Actually,' Eva's father responded, breaking the silence that had descended upon the table. 'I think that Eva and Nana were just going to bed as it's getting late.'

'Alright then,' the boy replied, undaunted, 'How about tomorrow then?'

'We'll see what tomorrow brings, shall we?' Mr Harrison said, not wanting to encourage the boy too much.

'Fine,' Charlie answered, before trotting off through the various tables. Then he turned and said in his cheery Liverpool accent, 'G'night.'

As Nana's father was tucking his daughter up in her bed she asked, 'Shall I pray that you find your New Testament, Daddy?'

'You could do,' her father answered, as he climbed onto the top bunk with his other Bible. 'I would love to get it back, wherever it has gone.'

Friends in First Class

On the Friday morning, Nana awoke with the excited anticipation of what another day, on the world's biggest ship, would bring.

She was disappointed at breakfast to find that Eva had slept in, but Charlie appeared again as bold as ever, asking Nana if she was free to play. Nana was still a little unsure of this rather cheeky boy. However, after prompting from her father, she agreed that if it was all right with Eva's parents, Eva and herself would spend some time with him later on. Charlie seemed pleased at the possibility of having a couple of playmates and disappeared with a big smile across his face.

'Now, Nana,' her father said as she finished her breakfast, 'you just remember to be careful when you are playing with Charlie. He may lead you into a bit of mischief.'

'Alright, Daddy,' his daughter answered, 'but I don't think that Eva and I will want to spend too much time with him. We want to play with Eva's teddy bear today.'

'Do you like adventure games?' Charlie asked the two friends, as he joined them later. Both girls looked up from playing with Eva's bear.

'What sort of adventure games?' Eva asked, with a disinterested air.

'Well,' Charlie replied, in a conspiratorial manner, 'I know how to get to some of the places on the ship you're not supposed to go.'

'What do you mean?' Nana asked.

'How would you like to see what it's like in first class?' Charlie replied. 'Or look at the boiler room where they make the steam to turn the ship's propellers?'

'The boiler room,' Nana retorted, wriggling her nose in disgust. 'Who would want to see the boiler room? It sounds dirty and boring!'

'You should see the men down there shovelling coal into gigantic boilers,' Charlie enthused. 'If you like, you can see all the ladders and small passageways throughout the ship too. I've explored 'em all. And,' he added triumphantly, 'I even know that the ship is on fire.'

'It's on fire!' both girls spoke in unison.

'Yes, it's on fire! I've seen it with my own eyes. In one of the bunkers where they store coal, there's a fire. The men down there are trying to shovel the coal around, and put water on it so that they can put the fire out.'

'Why do they have coal on a ship?' Eva asked, rather interested by Charlie's story.

'To heat the boilers, that make the steam, that works the engines, which turn the propellers, that push the ship through the water,' Charlie explained, with the apparent knowledge of a trained engineer.

'So why is the coal on fire?' Nana enquired, a little concerned.

'I dunno. I just saw some men shovelling it about and heard one of them saying they had to put the fire out and stop the coal from burning. It was pretty smelly and steamy down there. We could go and see what's going on if you like.'

'But are you allowed in those parts of the ship?' Eva enquired with a frown.

'No, of course not,' Charlie answered truthfully, 'but I've explored lots of places on this ship you're not supposed to. It's like a great big playground. So then, what part do you want to see first?'

'I'd love to see what it's like in first class,' Nana said enthusiastically, completely forgetting her father's advice about what kind of things Charlie might lead her into.

'Come on, then,' he said to the two girls, 'let's go.'

'But my parents told me I must tell them if I was going somewhere else,' Eva said, glancing at Nana.

'Oh, you'll not be gone long,' Charlie replied. 'I'll just show you first class and we'll be back in no time at all!' With that Charlie guided the two rather apprehensive girls out of the lounge they were playing in. He led them along a corridor that ran up the port side of the ship and past some second class cabins. Charlie stopped where two corridors met and cautiously looked round the corner to check no one was coming. All was quiet so he signalled for the two girls to follow him. They darted across the passageway and Charlie opened a door that had 'Crew Only' written across it. 'In here,' he said. The girls followed him through the door. 'No one, but the crew are allowed in 'ere,' Charlie said with a grin, but I've been all over this ship exploring like. I bet there's nowhere on this ship I 'aven't been,' he added.

Both girls looked at each other warily. Nana pulled Charlie's sleeve and said, 'I think maybe we should go back. I don't think my daddy would be pleased if he knew what we were doing.'

'But he ain't going to know, is he?' Charlie responded, wagging his finger in front of Nana's face to re-emphasise his point.

The two girls followed, hesitantly, as Charlie led them along more passageways and up and down several metal staircases. Both girls were beginning to wish they had just stayed where they were, playing with the bear.

Eventually, their guide stopped and pointed to a door that had a small circular window near the top of it. 'Wait here!' he ordered them. 'Through that door is first class. I'll just check it's safe.' The girls waited anxiously while Charlie stood on his tiptoes to peer through the window of the door. Then, turning to his companions he said, 'Get a move on, it's safe enough.' He pushed the door open and beckoned them to follow him. As they entered the room behind the door, Nana and Eva stood spellbound, gazing at the sumptuous luxury in which they found themselves.

'Wow!' Eva exclaimed. 'It really is beautiful.'

'Welcome to first class,' Charlie announced. 'Home of the top hats, ball gowns and millionaires!' quoting from a magazine he picked up on a previous visit to this part of the ship.

'Hello,' a voice spoke from a large chair that was partly hidden by the door Charlie was holding open. 'Where have you three young people come from?'

The children were startled by the sound of the voice. They turned in the direction from which it had come. There, confronting them, was a well-dressed man in his forties and sitting next to him a very pretty young lady, who was wearing an exquisite velvet dress trimmed with braid and covered in buttons.

'Mr and Mrs Astor,' Nana breathed, before catching herself.

'Ah,' said the man smiling. 'You see, Madeline, these youngsters know who we are, but we do not know who they are.'

The three children stood dumbfounded, staring at the couple who sat in front of them. Mr Astor smiled at Nana gently. 'How do you know who I am, young lady?' he asked.

The little girl blushed with embarrassment and gazed down at the plush carpet on which she was standing.

'Don't be afraid,' the man said. 'I just wanted to discover how you knew our names.'

'My daddy and I saw you get on the ship when we stopped in Cherb...Charbo...Cher...' her voice trailed away, as she continued to look at the floor in embarrassment.

'Cherbourg,' Mr Astor added, helpfully. 'Then why have you three come into this room through a door that says 'Crew only'. You're not members of the ship's crew, are you?' he asked, with a chuckle.

'We were just exploring the ship,' Charlie answered, rather sheepishly.

'Excellent, excellent,' Mr Astor enthused. 'I like young people with entrepreneurial spirits.'

'What does 'entrap, entrana... er that big word mean?' Eva asked.

'It means you have good ideas and get on and do them,' Mr Astor answered, rising from his seat and taking a couple of steps towards the children. 'So, where did you come from, to arrive here in first class?'

'Well, sir,' Charlie piped up, feeling a little more at ease. 'We are all from second class and I have brought these two girls here 'cause they wanted to see what it was like in first class.' He paused and added, 'Please, don't get them into trouble. It was all my fault really.'

'My dear,' Mr Astor said, motioning to his wife, 'we can show them around can't we?' Then turning to the children he said, 'Don't worry, we'll not get you into trouble. Come with us and we will give you a tour of the *Titanic's* finest first class accommodation. But before we do,' he added, 'what are your names?'

When all three had given their names Mr Astor added, 'I am very pleased to meet you. My name is John and this is my wife, Madeline.'

'Where would you like us to start?' he asked, as they began to walk through the magnificent lounge. 'I think we could start with the dining saloon and maybe get you three children a small snack of something.'

'Oh, yes, please,' Charlie spoke out, 'I'm starved!'

'But you can't be,' Eva retorted in embarrassment at Charlie's outspokenness. 'We've only just had lunch!'

'Come with us,' Mrs Astor spoke, quite amused at the children. 'I think you may prefer something from the confectionary shop.'

'What's a confectionary shop?' Nana questioned Eva under her breath.

'I'm not sure,' Eva whispered back shrugging her shoulders.

Madeline Astor smiled again as she overheard the children's hushed conversation.

'A confectionary shop is just a big word for a sweet shop. All children like sweet shops,' she explained.

'But we haven't any money,' Eva stated with a note of sadness in her voice.

'Oh, don't worry,' Mr Astor said. 'We can afford to buy a few sweets don't you agree dear?' he said glancing at his wife.

As the Astors led the way, the three children gazed in wide-eyed wonder at the grandeur of the rooms they passed through. Nana had to pinch herself to make sure

73

she was not dreaming. They were led through the first class library, this was lined with mahogany bookcases full of leather-bound books. Eva was amazed at how much grander this was to their own impressive second class library. From here they descended the most beautiful staircase they had ever seen in their lives. The girls stopped and gazed around them as the Astors continued on down the steps, chatting away to Charlie about various aspects of the ship's design. 'What's the matter?' Mr Astor called behind him, as he realised two of his new charges were no longer with him.

'It's just beautiful,' Nana sighed, as she stood gazing up at the great glass dome that towered high above her head. Her eye had caught sight of the brightness of the April sun, which was shining through the colourful mosaic of glass and steel.

'Look at that clock,' enthused Charlie, who was a bit disappointed that his position of chief guide had been usurped by these two adults. 'Does it really work?'

All five stood on the stairs staring at a large clock that had been set into an intricately carved mahogany surround. On either side of the clock face were two angels with wings.

'Oh, that is 'Honour and Glory crowning time.' That is what it is supposed to represent anyway,' Mr Astor told them.

Suddenly Eva noticed the time on the clock and interrupted with great alarm. 'Oh, no, look at the time! My parents will wonder where I am.'

With this, a cold shiver ran through Nana as she too realised that by now her father would be wondering where she was as well.

'Don't worry,' Mr Astor assured, 'I will come back with you and make sure you don't get into any trouble, but first let's go to the confectionary store!'

It was fifteen minutes later that the three rather apprehensive children were led by the Astors back to second class. The children followed them along the second class promenade deck, before descending the staircase that led down to the lounge where they had promised Mr Harrison they would stay. Each child carried a stick of bright pink candy floss in one hand and an ice cream in the other. Charlie had devoured most of his ice cream by the time they reached the lounge. However, the girls were taking their time savouring every lick. Mr Astor carried three large paper bags stuffed full with enough candy and treats to last each of the children the rest of the voyage. The sight of the Astors walking totally unconcerned through the second class area drew looks of surprise and amazement from the passengers who recognised them.

An agitated Mr Harrison was pacing up and down in the lounge when they arrived. He immediately began to berate his daughter about wandering off without telling him. He was in full flight when Mr Astor interrupted.

'Actually sir, it was entirely my fault,' he announced to the surprised Mr Harrison. 'May I introduce myself?

My name is John Jacob Astor.' Mr Harrison's jaw dropped open. 'You see,' he went on to explain, 'the children wanted to see what it was like in first class and I insisted on showing them round. I know I really should have got your permission first, but it was just a spur of the moment plan. I do hope that my wife and I have not caused you too much distress or concern?'

'No, er no, not at all, sir,' Eva's father stammered unable to fully grasp that his daughter and her friends had just been entertained by one of the world's richest men.

'In fact, we have brought you a little something in order to apologise for the worry we may have caused,' Mrs Astor kindly interrupted, handing over a rather large box of chocolates.

'Oh, thank you very much,' said Mr Harrison who had now been joined by his wife. 'There wasn't any need for you to do that.' Then turning to his wife he explained, 'Eva, Nana and their friend have been given a guided tour round the first class area of the ship by Mr and Mrs Astor.'

Eva's mother, realising now who the two beautifully dressed strangers were, curtsied politely and said, 'We are very pleased to make your acquaintance.'

Eva had to suppress a giggle at seeing her mother curtsying and trying to be so polite.

'We also have a little something for the parents of Nana and Charlie,' Mr Astor continued amicably.

'I'll give it to mine,' Charlie quickly replied, 'as my dad will probably be asleep.'

'That's fine,' Mrs Astor answered, being a little surprised at him being asleep so early in the afternoon. 'We wouldn't want to disturb him.'

'Oh, no,' Charlie answered guardedly, 'Dad usually sleeps most of the afternoon and Mum doesn't come out of the cabin much.'

'Does your father not keep well?' Mr Astor asked Charlie carefully.

'He's fine thanks,' Charlie replied, in a way that made it clear he did not wish to be asked any more questions.

'Hello, Nana,' the familiar voice of her father came from the entrance of the lounge.

'Oh, Daddy,' she said excitedly as she looked up at him. 'Mr and Mrs Astor have been showing Eva, Charlie and me around first class.'

'Really,' her father answered, looking at his daughter in an almost disbelieving way.

'Yes, that's right, and we hope that you did not mind,' Mr Astor spoke up.

Nana's father looked at the smartly dressed man and immediately recognised him.

'W...well, thank you very much, Mr Astor,' he said falteringly. 'I am sure the children will have been delighted with that.'

'I do hope so, but my wife and I are aware they have been gone for a while, so we have a little something to appease you with.' His wife handed over another large box of chocolates to Mr Harper.

'These are for you and your wife,' she added. 'They are Belgian chocolates. The best you can buy. At least that's what they claim in the confectionary store!'

Nana's father took the box of chocolates, still wearing a bemused expression on his face. 'That really is most kind. My wife went to heaven six years ago, but I shall enjoy the chocolates myself.'

Mr and Mrs Astor were a little taken aback to realise that Nana had no mother. Mrs Astor recovered herself quickly and said, 'We are so sorry about your wife, but, yes, please do enjoy the chocolates yourself.'

'My mummy's in a beautiful place in heaven,' Nana interrupted, in her unashamed way. 'My daddy says it's even nicer than where you both stay in first class.'

'Yes, I am sure it is,' Mr Astor responded, glad at the little girl's interruption, which helped to relieve the embarrassment he was feeling.

'In fact,' Nana continued, 'Daddy even said, when he saw you both get on the ship, that he'd like to speak to you about the riches of heaven.'

'Oh,' said Mr Astor, as if not sure what he should say. He then continued, 'Many people like to speak to me about the riches of earth. However, no one has, as yet, spoken to me about the riches of heaven, whatever they are.'

Mr Harper, recovering from the rather forthright manner his daughter had addressed such an eminent person added, 'I must apologise for my daughter's bluntness, but I am a preacher of the gospel and love to share with people how they can be rich in God, by having faith in our Lord Jesus Christ.'

'Don't apologise for your daughter,' Mr Astor said good-humouredly. 'I like a child who can speak their mind. Now, I do have to admit that, rich as I may be, I am not aware that I can be rich in God, but I guess that you believe that is a most important thing?'

'Yes, indeed I do,' Mr Harper replied with a smile. 'You see, the Lord Jesus told a story in Luke's gospel about a rich man who had lots of money and built great barns on his farm, but never thought about God. Then one day he died and left everything behind and the Lord Jesus said, "So is he that lays up treasure for himself and is not rich towards God". You see he left everything in this life behind and had nothing for the next.'

Mr and Mrs Astor looked at each other thoughtfully. Then Mr Astor, turning back to look at Mr Harper said, 'I remember as a teenager reading the sermons of Charles Spurgeon. Didn't he say something similar?'

'Yes, he did. I've read many of those messages myself too,' Mr Harper replied.

'I must admit I have given little thought to God and heaven throughout my life. Maybe it's something I shouldn't have neglected.' Mr Astor paused then looked at his wife again and said, 'But for now I think that it is time we went back to our own area. I know that the White Star company do not take kindly to second class passengers entering first class accommodation, so perhaps they may be upset with first class venturing into second class.' Then turning to Nana's father once again he added, 'Perhaps we may be able to talk about these interesting things another time?'

'Yes I hope so,' replied Mr Harper.

'Oh, I almost forgot,' Mrs Astor broke in. 'We have three bags of candy and chocolates for the children.' Then taking them from her husband's hand she bent down to pass them out to the three eager children. Then she added with a smile, 'Don't eat them all at once or you may make yourselves sick.'

The Captain and the Coal

The next morning brought more excitement for Nana and Eva. They were standing out on the deck enjoying the breeze when they saw an older man, with a white beard dressed in a very fine uniform, walking down the deck in their direction. He was accompanied by seven or eight other men all in smart uniforms and wearing very official-looking peak hats. Eva's father was nearby and sensing that both girls were puzzled at the group who were walking towards them said, 'That's the ship's captain making his daily tour of inspection with his senior crew members.'

'The Captain!' both girls said at the same time.

'Yes, his name is Captain Smith and every day he and his senior officers walk round the ship to ensure everything is as it should be,' explained Mr Harrison.

By this time, the Captain and his various crew members had arrived at where the two girls were standing. The Captain noticed they were staring at him and said jovially, 'Hello there, and who are these two pretty young ladies travelling on board my ship?'

Nana, although not really scared of him, suddenly went shy as she looked up at his kindly, whiskered cheeks that reminded her a little of Father Christmas.

'I'm Eva Harrison and this is my friend Nana Harper,' Eva replied for them both.

The Captain nodded and still with a smile asked, 'Why are you both travelling to America?'

'I am going to Pittsburgh with my mum and dad to start a chemist's shop,' Eva replied confidently.

'And what about you, young lass?' Captain Smith enquired, as he bent down closer to Nana.

'I am travelling with my daddy to America so that he can tell the people there about how much God loves them,' Nana answered.

'Is that so,' the Captain said as he straightened himself. 'So both your parents will be busy. One mending people's bodies and the other mending people's souls!'

Just then Nana's father arrived and turning to him she said excitedly, 'This is Captain Smith.'

'Ah,' said the Captain, looking at Mr Harper, 'so you are the preacher?'

'Yes,' Nana's father answered, with a bemused expression.

The Captain, seeing the look of surprise on his face, explained, 'Your daughter has been telling me that you are going to America to tell the people there of God's love, so I surmised that you must be a preacher.'

'Oh, I see,' Mr Harper replied, his countenance clearing. 'Yes, that is correct. I am going to Chicago to preach the gospel.'

'We had a religious revival in Wales ten years ago,' one of the men in uniform spoke out.

'This is Mr Lowe, my fifth officer,' the Captain added, introducing the officer. 'As you may have gathered from his accent, he is Welsh.'

Mr Harper turned to the Welsh officer and said, 'Yes, I heard about that revival and was thrilled to hear of so many turning to Christ for salvation. I understand that, as a result, all the churches and chapels in Wales grew much bigger.'

'It was amazing,' Mr Lowe continued. 'Although I was just a teenager, there were people queuing to get into churches at that time.'

'Perhaps some of our trimmers and boiler men should attend church more often,' the Captain replied jauntily. 'I am sure it would do them good and clean up their often rather colourful language.'

The Captain's officers all laughed at his comment.

'Excuse me,' Eva's father interrupted, 'but my daughter has been asking me lots of questions about the ship and I am just wondering if you might be kind enough to answer them for her.'

'Why, of course,' responded the Captain, turning his full attention to Eva. 'Now, what would you like to know?'

'Go on, Eva,' her father encouraged, 'this is the man who is in charge of the ship and will know everything about it.'

The Captain answered with a laugh, 'I am the Captain and know a fair bit about the ship, but I have with me, Mr Andrews, the designer and builder of the ship. He may be able to answer some of your questions better than I can.' He turned to introduce a tall, good-looking man in his early forties, wearing a Macintosh coat.

'What would you like to know?' Mr Andrews asked, in an Irish accent, as he bent down to the level of the two girls.

'How big is this ship, and is it really the biggest in the world?' Eva asked enthusiastically.

Mr Andrews answered with a smile, 'Yes, it is the biggest ship in the world at the moment. It is just slightly larger than its sister ship, the *Olympic*. The *Titanic* is eight hundred and eighty-two-and-a-half feet long and weighs forty-eight thousand tons. It is a very big ship, in fact,' he added proudly. 'It is the largest thing made by man ever to move in the world.'

'And how fast will it travel?' Eva added, enjoying every minute of speaking to the man who had built the wonderful vessel that she was travelling on.

'About twenty-five knots, at full speed, and when it is full it can carry three thousand people in comfort. However, on this trip there are only around two thousand two hundred on board.'

'And is it really, um—er—um—er, unsinkable?' she added, unsure of how to phrase the question.

'Well, I don't think that you can ever call a ship unsinkable,' Mr Andrews replied. 'But I believe that this ship comes as close as possible to that.' Then, looking at the Captain and his officers, he said to Eva with a smile, 'With all your questions, I think, young lady, you could be a ship builder!'

'Thank you for answering my daughter's questions,' Mr Harrison said.

'My pleasure,' Mr Andrews responded.

'Well, gentlemen,' Captain Smith said, with an air of authority, 'we need to continue our inspection.' Turning to the two girls and their fathers he added, 'Have a pleasant and enjoyable trip. Good day.'

As the Captain and his officers moved away, the girls noticed Charlie sauntering along the deck, his hands in his pockets. He was heading in their direction, but was trying to create an appearance that he did not care where he was going.

As soon as the girls saw him, they excitedly tried to tell him that they had just been talking with the Captain and the designer of the ship. At first Charlie was unable to make head nor tail of what they were trying to tell him. 'Slow down,' he said. 'Who've you seen?'

'The Captain,' blurted out Nana.

'And the designer of the ship, he's called Mr Andrews,' Eva added.

'Where are they now?' Charlie asked excitedly. 'I'd like to talk to them too.'

'They went down there,' Eva said, pointing in the direction of one of the staircases. Charlie headed in the same direction.

He returned a few minutes later appearing rather dejected. He hadn't been able to find them. He assumed they must have gone through one of the 'crew only' doors. He knew it would be no use chasing after them down one of the corridors behind those doors. He would only be sent back.

That afternoon Charlie asked the girls if they wanted to see the men shovelling the coal into the boilers down below in the boiler room. He was also keen that they should see the new, shiny engines that he had been so impressed with. The girls didn't find the thought of such noisy and dirty places very appealing, but remembering how well the adventure the day before had turned out, they agreed to go with him.

So off the three adventurers went, this time slipping unobserved into the third class part of the ship and through one of the 'crew only' doors. As they gently closed the door behind them, Charlie said with a smile, 'Look at this,' and pointed to a notice on the back of the door that said 'This door must be kept locked at all times.'

'Then why is the door not locked?' Eva asked him.

'I dunno. When I tried it three days ago it was open and so thought it might be open today as well. I guess that someone has forgotten to lock it. Let's go this way. I'll show you where the boilers are and where they store the coal. There are mountains of it,' he enthused, waving his hands animatedly.

The two girls obediently followed Charlie as he led them along a narrow passageway and down a spiral staircase. Once at the bottom, they found themselves in a larger passageway illuminated by electric lights that were positioned at intervals along the roof. After dodging in and out of various doorways, Charlie led them up another iron staircase. 'Quiet now,' he said, raising his finger to his lips. 'This leads to a metal walkway above the boiler room where we can watch the men filling the boilers with coal. It's a bit hot and noisy so watch out.'

Charlie carefully opened the door in front of them and bending low they crawled onto a metal grid-like walkway. It allowed you to see right through to where the men were working in the boiler room below. Charlie sat down and then manoeuvred into a lying position, before motioning for the girls to do the same. All three lay as still as possible, peering down at the hive of activity that was going on underneath them. They saw barrel loads of coal being dumped in front of men dressed in dirty white overalls. These men then picked it up on shovels and threw it into huge boilers that looked to Nana and Eva like giant metal pots that had been laid on their side. Every now and again someone with a large metal rod would close up the door of a full boiler and open up a new one that required more coal. As the man with the rod was opening and closing the boiler doors, the men shovelling the coal would stand up, stretch their backs and wipe their brows with what seemed to be large handkerchiefs tied loosely round their necks. Then, once again, they would commence shovelling coal into the newly opened boiler.

'I wouldn't want to do that job,' Eva spoke into Nana's ear.

'Me neither,' Nana answered. 'It's far too dirty!'

'They have to do it all the time,' Charlie told them.

Like Charlie had warned them, they too were beginning to feel some of the heat that the men below constantly experienced.

'I'll show you the engine room now,' Charlie mouthed slowly, wiping the perspiration from his forehead.

All three carefully clambered back along the metal walkway and through the door. Charlie led them once again through the maze of narrow passageways. They ducked in and out of openings and doorways, checking each time that the coast was clear before moving on. The two girls' initial reservations about such an adventure quickly disappeared as they enjoyed the excitement of following their leader through the bowels of the ship. Suddenly, at one of the passage intersections, Charlie stopped dead. He swiftly turned and hustled the girls back into the alcove of a doorway. 'Quiet!' he whispered in urgent tones. The three children stood still. Above the drone of the ship's engines they could hear the sound of approaching footsteps. They held their breath, hearts pounding. Then with great relief they watched as a tall young man in a navy blue uniform passed them by. He seemed fully occupied, as he scribbled away with a pencil on a clipboard which he held in his hand. Almost in unison, the children let out a sigh and began to breathe normally again. 'That was close,' Charlie whispered excitedly. 'I've been down 'ere twice and that's the first person I've seen. Mind you, I wouldn't want to be down 'ere when the men's shifts change 'cos this is the way to their cabins and they all come crowding up 'ere.'

As they got closer to the engine rooms, the noise intensified. Charlie led the two girls through a large door and onto another metal walkway that looked out, this time, over the huge engines of the *Titanic*. The noise was so intense that both girls cupped their hands over their ears in an attempt to block out the deafening sound. Standing, leaning against a railing, the three looked out over a tangle of gleaming brass pipes, noisy pistons and powerful pumps. The engines seemed to work away almost effortlessly. Occasionally, wisps of steam shot out of valves situated around the perimeter of each engine. These made a loud hiss which caused the girls to jump with surprise each time. Several men were busy checking dials, gauges and other gadgets and Nana wondered how they could work in such noisy conditions without getting a terrific headache. The girls remained with their hands cupped over their ears. Charlie was unable to make himself heard, so he pulled on the girl's arms and signalled for them to follow him back through the door. It was only once the door had closed behind them and the great noise had died away, that the girls felt able to remove their hands from their ears.

'How can those men work in all that noise?' Nana asked incredulously. 'It's so loud.'

'I guess you get used to it,' Charlie answered, shrugging his shoulders. 'My dad says you can get used to most things over time,' then pausing he added, 'except drink.'

'What do you mean, "except drink?"' Eva questioned.

'My dad's an alcoholic,' Charlie answered. 'That's why you never see him about like you do your parents. He's nearly always drunk and my mum is too ashamed or scared to come out of her cabin in case he does something stupid. We're going to America to start a new life where Mum hopes she can get Dad back to how he was before he started to drink. I don't think it'll work. I can barely remember my father being sober at all. He's just never got used to the drink, I guess.'

Both girls looked at Charlie, unable to find suitable words to reply to this explanation about his father.

'I think maybe we ought to go back now,' Eva said, changing the subject.

'Let's just see if the fire is still burning in the coal bunker,' Charlie suggested. 'It's not far.' Once again the two girls followed their leader as he led them around areas of the vast ship that most passengers would never see. Eventually, the children arrived at a door that simply had written across it, 'Reserve Coal Bunker – Boiler Room 6.'

'How do you know your way around so well?' Nana asked.

'I 'ave a good sense of direction,' Charlie replied. 'At least that's what ma mum says. Once I've been somewhere, I can always find me way back.'

Cautiously, Charlie looked through the window of the door before opening it and the three of them entered into a large dirty room that smelt of sulphur. Inside were huge bunkers containing piles of coal. These piles rose like large black mountains high up the sides of the bunkers. 'Must 'ave put the fire out,' Charlie said with a disappointed look. 'It was down there and men were shovelling the burning coal out into barrows and taking it to the boilers to use it up first.'

'So there really was a fire down here?' Eva said in a surprised tone.

'Oh, yes,' answered Charlie, 'It was in that bunker there,' he said, pointing through a doorway that obviously led to another area of coal storage. 'I say, I'd love to climb up those coal mountains, wouldn't you?'

The two girls pulled faces of obvious disagreement before Eva answered, 'Certainly not! Why ever would we want to climb up one of those dirty stacks of coal?'

'Just for the fun of it,' Charlie replied.

'Anyway, it might be dangerous,' Eva retorted.

'Na! It's not dangerous,' Charlie exclaimed running towards the nearest large pile of coal, 'Watch!'

Before the two girls had a chance to stop him, Charlie was climbing up the coal stack, his feet sliding on the loose coal. Up he went, higher and higher. The coal dislodged by his hands and feet rolled down the stack behind him, landing just in front of the two girls.

'Do be careful, Charlie,' Nana called, as he slipped and slid about.

'I am,' Charlie panted back, as he continued his upward progress. Eventually, in triumph, he reached the top of the pile towering above the girls. 'There,' he said, with an air of great pride, 'Made it!'

'Oi! What are you children doing down here?' a voice called from further along the coal bunker.

Both girls swung round. There, moving quickly towards them, was the man in the navy suit whom they had hidden from earlier. Charlie saw him too and trying to run down the pile of coal, lost his footing and came tumbling down the steep slope. He landed heavily at the bottom, a dirty, blackened individual, coal dust covering his clothes, skin and hair. 'Quickly, run!' he said, picking himself up off the floor and bolting through the coal store to the nearest door.

The two girls started running behind him as the voice of the man cried out, 'Stop! Stop! You three, stop now!'

As they ran, they could hear the footsteps of the man pounding up behind them. Suddenly Charlie shouted, 'Through here.' He dived off to his right and through another open doorway. The girls followed quickly behind him, just pausing in time to see the man with the clipboard slide on the coal dust and tumble to the ground. Up yet another narrow passageway, the two girls ran, puffing and panting, following Charlie who looked like he had fallen into a pot of black paint.

'Come back!' the man's voice echoed through the passageway, but from further away this time.

'Keep running,' panted Charlie, as they ran round the corner of yet another passageway and towards a staircase. Up the steps Charlie flew, leaving the two girls puffing in his wake. He turned right along another passageway before stopping outside the door to a room that had a notice saying 'Laundry' on it. Charlie tried the handle and the door opened. The girls caught up with him and the three stepped inside before quietly closing the door behind them. All three stood leaning against the door, puffing hard and listening for any sounds of their pursuer.

After what seemed like an age, Eva looked at Charlie and began to giggle. He did look a state covered as he was from head to foot in coal dust. Charlie laughed too, but more with a sense of relief that they had not been caught than anything else.

'Do you know where we are?' Nana enquired of Charlie expectantly.

'No, I 'aven't a clue,' he admitted honestly, 'but if we keep going up whenever we find a staircase we will eventually get back to the passenger areas.'

'What if we end up back in first class?' Eva asked.

Charlie paused thoughtfully before answering, 'We will just have to tell them we have come to say thank you to Mr and Mrs Astor for the candy they gave us.'

'What! With you looking like that?' Eva replied in horror.

'And that would be telling a lie too,' Nana added, 'and that's wrong.'

'Okay, it was just an idea,' Charlie scoffed.

After some discussion all three left the security of the now rather dusty laundry room and headed out once more along the many passages that dissected the ship below passenger levels. Eventually, after a near miss with another crew member, the three children opened a door that said 'Lower Deck G – Third Class Accommodation'. From here they quickly and carefully made their way up to the third class promenade deck. How glad they were to be out once again in the fresh air. Even Charlie did not mind the strange looks that many of the passengers gave him as he made his way back to his own cabin to get washed and cleaned up. Nana and Eva were also relieved to be in part of the ship where they could not get into trouble.

Later that night, as her father was tucking her up in bed, Nana confessed the details of the day's adventure to him. 'You see, Nana,' her father replied, 'following Charlie could have resulted in a lot of trouble and bother. As a Christian you have to be prepared to say no when someone wants to lead you in the wrong direction. It's not always easy but Christians must live for the Lord.' Then, as he bent and gently kissed her, he chuckled and said, 'I'd like to have seen Charlie though! He must have been a sight all covered in coal dust. Good night.'

Sorry!

On Sunday morning Nana woke as usual to find her father on his knees in prayer. 'Will we be going to church today?' she asked from the warmth and comfort of her bed

Her father turned and slowly rose from his position of prayer. 'Well, there is no morning service, but Mr Collings tells me that he has gained permission to conduct some hymn singing in the dining saloon this evening, so we can go there. Otherwise, I think we will just have a quiet day and think about the Lord Jesus and how he died for us, so that we could go to heaven.'

'Daddy,' the little girl answered, as the morning sun flashed in through the porthole and lit up her chestnut curls, 'I do like thinking about heaven because Mummy is there.'

'Heaven is a lovely thought, especially because the Lord Jesus Christ is there. However, he is watching very carefully over us down here and promises to always be with us. In fact, when we are Christians, he is with us in everything we do in life, whether it be a difficult thing or just something that we enjoy.'

Before Nana and her father went down for breakfast they read together the well-known passage in the Bible, Psalm 23.

'The Lord is my shepherd I shall not want.
He maketh me to lie down in green pastures:
He leadeth me beside the still waters.
He restoreth my soul:
He leadeth me in the paths of righteousness
for His name's sake.
Yea though I walk through the valley of the
shadow of death,
I will fear no evil:
For Thou art with me:
Thy rod and thy staff comfort me.
Thou preparest a table before me in the presence of
mine enemies:
Thou anointest my head with oil;
My cup runneth over.
Surely goodness and mercy shall follow me
all the days of my life:
And I will dwell in the house of the Lord for ever.'

With it being Sunday, everything on board the ship was much quieter than usual. The continual noise of chattering, that usually filled the dining saloon, seemed oddly hushed as the various passengers sat down to breakfast.

Mr Harper, having enjoyed a good breakfast, spent some time talking with Mr and Mrs Collings. Nana found Eva and the two girls kept themselves occupied reading books and drawing pictures. They had determined that, as it was Sunday, they would keep themselves well out of trouble.

Charlie came to find them and, having been told that they had no intention of going on any exploratory trips today, suggested a game of hoopla. Nana thought a game of hide and seek was probably more appropriate. They decided, again at Nana's suggestion, to call it lost and found, after the Bible story of the Good Shepherd and the lost sheep. Eva added a rule for Charlie's benefit which was that they could hide only in the second class part of the ship. Even so, Charlie usually found the best hiding places. However, Nana was delighted when she hid herself under a fixed bench and two ladies seeing her, sat down on the bench spreading out their long skirts so as to completely hide her. The other two just could not find her and, after a long search, Nana gave herself up and was voted the lost and found champion of the day.

In the afternoon, Nana and her father decided to go for a walk along the deck. Eva said she would stay in the library and finish off some drawings she'd started earlier. She was having a go at designing her own ship and was hoping to bump into Mr Andrews again, so that she could show him her efforts.

Out on the deck, the sun was shining brightly. Nana and her father looked out at the sea from between the lifeboats that hung in their davits, along both sides of the deck. The breeze was stiff and the air was much cooler than they had known it throughout the trip. Mr Harper shivered in mock fun at the cold air that hit him.

'It's not that cold, Daddy,' Nana piped up, as she looked up at her father. 'In fact, the sea looks almost warm enough to swim in.'

'Brrrrrrrrr,' her father said, as he turned the collar of his coat up to keep out the breeze.

'Mr Harper?' a voice came from behind them. 'You are Mr Harper, aren't you?'

They both turned round to see a tall young man with a mop of curly blond hair coming towards them. He was wearing a long knee-length coat which covered his thin frame.

'Yes, I am Mr Harper,' Nana's father answered. 'Do I know you?'

'No sir, you don't,' the young man answered, 'but we have met before.'

'You're one of the rough men who pushed my daddy the other day,' Nana spoke, before the man could say anything more.

'Yes,' he answered, as he lowered his head and looked down at his shoes, ashamed to face the two standing before him. 'I was one of those men who bumped into you the other day. I want to say that I am sorry for taking this out of your pocket.' He placed his hand into his own pocket, pulled something out and handed it to Mr Harper.

'My New Testament!' exclaimed Mr Harper, with delight. Taking the precious little book, he enquired, 'But why did you take it?'

The young man, without making any eye-contact with the preacher answered, 'I thought it might have been a wallet, but when I got back into our cabin with my friends, I found it was your Bible.' He paused, as if not knowing what to say next, then carried on. 'I was so disgusted, I threw the book against the cabin wall, but it fell back onto my bed and opened at some words you had underlined. I read them. They said: "The thief cometh to steal and kill and destroy; I am come that they might have life, and that they might have it more abundantly".'

'That's right,' Mr Harper replied, smiling at the young man. 'You must have been reading the words of the Lord Jesus which are written in John Chapter 10.

The young man blushed deeply before responding, 'I read those words and felt awful because I realised that I was a thief and was destroying, not just my own life but the lives of other people as well. It suddenly dawned on me too, that I would end up in big trouble if I carried on.' The young man, clearly feeling the need to relieve himself of his burden, continued. 'When I boarded with my friends at Queenstown, we all decided that we would try and slip out of third class and run through the ship bumping into folks and take their wallets out of their jackets, or purses out of their handbags. It's been my way of life since I left school, but your little book made me feel different about things. I have wanted to come and give it back to you since Thursday, but my friends wouldn't let me in case you reported us. I just feel so terrible,' he finished, with tears welling up in his eyes.

'May I say a couple of things to you?' Mr Harper asked, in a kindly and forgiving tone. 'Firstly, let's find a seat so we can speak more comfortably.' The two made their way towards a seat that was situated behind the last of the ship's great funnels. As they sat down, they looked straight out over the stern of the ship and across the frothing sea, which was being stirred up by the *Titanic's* three enormous propellers.

Nana, deciding that it could be a long conversation, asked her daddy if she could go and join Eva in the library.

'That's an excellent idea,' he replied. 'I shall come and find you in a few minutes.'

Mr Harper looked at the young man who still gazed at the floor, and spoke saying, 'I would like to say how very grateful I am that you had the courage to own up and give me back my little Testament, but you know I don't think it was just chance that you took my New Testament. When the book opened up at that verse you quoted to me, it was God speaking to you. His Holy Spirit has convicted you that what you have been doing is wrong. You have done a good thing in putting right what you did wrong against me. But your sins are against God and you need to confess them to him.' Mr Harper paused, waiting for some reaction from the young man.

The young man replied, 'Does that mean I have to leave my friends and stop the stealing and give back the things I've taken?

'That's right. You need to totally forsake your old life, make amends where you can and start a new life with the Lord Jesus Christ.'

'But I am so afraid of my friends.'

'Yes, sometimes being afraid of what our friends say and do is a very hard thing to overcome, but he that is able to save you, is also able to keep you.'

'I don't think I could ever become a Christian. As I've already said, my friends don't even know that I was coming to speak to you. I was going to tell them that I had thrown your book overboard.'

'You need to tell them the truth.'

His face crumpled at the thought. He composed himself and sat still for a short while, gazing out to sea as if hypnotised by its vast expanse. 'But you don't understand,' he said looking into the preacher's eyes for the first time. 'My friends would hate me and leave me. In fact, they would probably kill me.'

Mr Harper went on to explain, 'When a person knows the Lord Jesus as Saviour, the Bible says that the Holy Spirit comes to live in them and we have this promise that, "greater is he that is in you than he that is in the world." What you need to do is to say sorry for your sins and ask Jesus to save you. He will do this because he died on the cross to take your sins away and he will give you this abundant life and help you overcome your fear of your friends.'

'I need to think about it,' the young man said, standing up. 'It's just such a big decision.'

'You're right,' Mr Harper said, standing too. 'It's such a big decision. It will be the biggest one you ever make.' Then pausing, he said, 'Just don't put it off too long.'

'Thank you for forgiving me,' the man said, brightening slightly. 'I do feel a little better.'

'Here, take this.' Mr Harper took out of his pocket one of the other Bibles he had with him and handed it to him.

'No, no, sir, I can't take that.'

'You can. It's a gift, just like God's offer of salvation. You may need it some day.'

The young man, hesitantly, put out his hand to take it. He then thanked Mr Harper and walked slowly away along the deck.

Mr Harper watched him disappear and then silently prayed for him, before going to find Nana in the library.

'Daddy,' quizzed Nana, when they resumed their walk on deck, 'did you tell the man about the Lord Jesus?'

'Yes, I did, my dear,'

'Did he ask him to be his Saviour?'

'No, he didn't.'

'Why not?'

'People have many reasons,' her father answered simply, but sadly. 'With him, it was his friends and what they would think or say if his life was changed by the power of Jesus Christ.'

Iceberg!

'Oh hear us when we cry to thee
For those in peril on the sea.'

The words of the hymn drifted from the second class dining saloon. Little Nana had been allowed to stay up late and attend the service. She was delighted when Mr Collings, who had recovered from his cold, singled her out for special attention telling everyone how she had fallen at his feet as they waited to board the ship. He had then asked her if she had a favourite hymn, and without hesitation, she said, 'Jesus loves me this I know for the Bible tells me so.' Her father and many others smiled as the little voice called up from among the crowd. She had enjoyed the time of singing with other passengers.

Now, it was just after 10.30 pm as she skipped lightly down the corridor towards her cabin still humming. She yawned as she waited for her father to open the door with his key.

'You're tired,' her father said, as he held the door open.

'Not really, Daddy,' she replied, as she danced inside the cabin. 'It's just that my mouth is tired from all that singing.' Then she said excitedly, 'I'm glad we sang my favourite hymn!'

Her father smiled as he helped her get ready for bed. He tucked her up before kneeling beside her to pray. When he'd finished praying, he looked at her peaceful face, her eyes were still closed in prayer. She opened them and looked at her father sleepily. 'Goodnight, Daddy,' she whispered, turned over and fell straight to sleep. Mr Harper reflected how good it was to be a young child, without a care in the world and having the love of God in your heart.

Mr Harper was in his bunk, hands behind his head and with his Bible lying open across his chest. He had been thinking about the young man who had returned his New Testament and the view he had seen when speaking to him. Sea, sea and more sea! Nothing but sea in every direction wherever you looked. He glanced down at his Bible and read the verse once again that had captured his soul just a few minutes before. 'And I saw a new heaven and a new earth; and there was no more sea.' 'Yes,' he thought to himself. 'How wonderful heaven will be with no sea to divide peoples, nations and continents!'

It was then that he felt it! A vibration! A strange gentle shaking that seemed to reverberate right through the ship. Not strong, but enough to cause the light fittings to shake and the water in his glass to swish about. It lasted only a few seconds before dying away, but some sixth sense told him that all was not right. Jumping down from his bunk, he went to the window and gazed out into the darkness of the night.

That was when he saw what he thought was a giant white sail passing very close to the ship. It was lit up by the numerous lights shining out from the *Titanic*'s many portholes. 'A ship,' he immediately thought. 'A sailing ship! We have hit a sailing ship. That's what caused the vibration.' He waited, as he felt the great ship's engines slow before finally stopping.

Leaving his daughter sleeping peacefully, he left the cabin and went out into the corridor. It was pretty much deserted as he made his way towards the dining saloon. A lady poked her head round from a cabin door and enquired, 'What is wrong?'

'I'm not sure,' he answered. 'I am going to find out.'

Entering the dining saloon, he encountered a number of men and women all talking excitedly. 'Yes, it was huge, like a mountain of ice,' someone said.

'Apparently one of the crew saw lots of ice fall on the foredeck at the front of the ship,' another exclaimed.

'You can't see it now though. It has floated past the ship.'

'Was it an iceberg? Did we hit it?'

The conversation continued.

'Oh, yes,' another answered, 'but I wouldn't worry about it, as I doubt it would be able to damage this ship.'

'Did you see it?' someone enquired of Mr Harper, seeing him enter the room.

'Yes,' he said, 'but when I looked out of the porthole I thought it was a sailing ship.'

'I guess it could have looked like that from inside,' someone answered. 'Still nothing to worry about, is there?' he finished.

A steward came down the staircase and into the saloon. 'Steward,' a lady called out, attracting his attention. 'Have we really hit an iceberg?' she questioned eagerly.

'There is talk of an iceberg, ma'am,' he answered. 'But I am sure it's nothing too serious. I suggest you all go back to your cabins and have a good night's sleep.'

'Why is it so hard to get anyone to give us any information?' another asked.

Mr Harper walked thoughtfully back to his cabin. He felt uneasy in the presence of people who were overconfident in the ship. It was no good thing to be too confident in man's ability. He had often seen in his ministry in Glasgow, how easily man's confidence could be shattered and broken. He had witnessed men with important jobs and good homes who had been broken by an addiction to alcohol. They had thought that they had everything and had then succumbed to the terrible scourge of drink. He had seen overconfident public figures who had thought they were invincible, brought to ruin by some sin in their lives. Yes, he knew the dangers all too well of man's overconfidence and reliance on himself and not in the great and unchangeable God.

'If we have hit an iceberg,' he reasoned, once back in his cabin, 'the ship will have been damaged in some way despite its great strength and size.' Once more Mr Harper went to the Lord in prayer. He sought wisdom so that he would be able to point others to the only one in whom people can have absolute confidence.

After about twenty minutes, there came a knock on his door. Opening it, he found Mr Collings standing there in his dressing gown and slippers. 'Listen!' he said, with a sense of alarm in his voice, 'Did you know that the ship has hit an iceberg?'

'Yes, I saw it go past my window.'

'I think the ship is badly damaged,' Mr Collings responded. 'The crew are considering uncovering the lifeboats. I just thought I would come to your cabin so that we could pray together about the situation.'

'Yes,' Mr Harper replied, 'I think that would be the very best thing to do.'

Both men knelt down in the cabin where Nana still slept soundly, unaware of the drama that was rapidly unfolding all around her. They prayed earnestly to God for wisdom and grace to face whatever might happen in the coming hours. They shook hands then Mr Collings left to rejoin his wife in their cabin.

Mr Harper took down his old, large Bible from his bunk and flicking through its pages came to a verse, 'Thou wilt keep him in perfect peace whose mind is stayed on thee.'

'Yes, Lord,' he prayed, 'may my mind this night be stayed on thee, that I might know thy peace and show it to others.'

Mr Harper once more went outside the cabin. Was it him or was the floor sloping very slightly? He was not sure, but thought that maybe the ship had a slight list to starboard. Again he made his way down to the dining saloon.

'Are they really going to lower the lifeboats?' a lady asked a male passenger as he came down the staircase.

'They are uncovering them up on the promenade deck,' he answered soberly. 'I think that we might be in a tight spot. It seems that the ship is holed and letting in water.'

'What are the crew telling us to do?' another enquired.

'Nothing,' he retorted, 'nothing. I can't get anyone to tell me what we should do other than stay in our cabins!'

Mr Harper pushed through the doors and ran up the stairs to the promenade deck where the lifeboats were slung. Here he found lots of passengers milling about watching the crew members uncover the lifeboats, before swinging them out from the ship over the sea.

'Excuse me,' he said to a man who seemed to be in charge of preparing the lifeboats for service. 'What is the situation?'

The officer, turning and recognising him from his meeting with the Captain, took him aside.

'You're a minister. You may be needed tonight, I don't know,' he confided. 'The ship is sinking by the head and has only about an hour left before it goes down. Captain Smith has ordered the boats uncovered and slung out ready to be filled with women and children.'

Mr Harper, shocked at what he had just heard, composed himself and then asked, 'Is there anything I can do to help?'

'Not at the moment but,' the officer placed his gloved hand to his mouth and whispered, 'as I said, you may be needed later as there is not enough room for everyone in the lifeboats.' A look of desperation came over the officer's face as he concluded, 'Who'd have ever thought that the unsinkable *Titanic* would sink because of a lump of ice!'

Mr Harper started to walk quietly back towards his cabin, when another voice arrested his progress. 'John,' it called out. He turned to see Eva's father chasing after him.

'John,' he repeated, 'they tell me the boat is sinking and that they will be putting the women and children off in the lifeboats.'

'That's what they have told me as well,' he answered.

'But there aren't enough lifeboats for everyone on board,' Mr Harrison responded.

'I know that, but thank God there is the lifeboat of Salvation available for all who trust Christ as Saviour,' Mr Harper replied.

'Listen,' Mr Harrison said, 'I have never really been too interested in religion and church services, but I may come and speak to you later tonight. Right now I want to get Esther and Eva into a lifeboat.'

'Yes, I want to do the same with Nana, but after that I'd be glad to point you to the Saviour.'

'Later then,' Mr Harrison said as he hurried away.

Mr Harper took another look around him at the crew busily uncovering the lifeboats. He noted the increasing number of passengers who were appearing on the deck. He'd seen enough and hastily continued his way back to the cabin. Here he found his daughter still sleeping peacefully.

'Nana,' he called gently, 'Nana, you need to get up for your daddy.' The little girl stirred and settled back into her blankets. 'Nana,' he said again a little louder, 'Nana, you must wake up for me, darling.'

Her eyes opened, as she sleepily asked, 'What's wrong, Daddy?'

'There is a problem with the ship, little one,' he said cautiously, 'and I need you to get up and get dressed as quickly as you can.'

The little girl snuggled into her bed again and hugged her pillow, 'Just a little longer, Daddy.'

'No! Now!' Her father's words this time came with authority and urgency and Nana knew that something was seriously wrong.

'What is it, Daddy? What's wrong with the ship?' she enquired, as she sat herself up in bed.

'We have hit something and the ship is leaking,' he tried to explain simply. 'You are going to go for a row in a little boat.'

'Oh,' she answered, with a sparkle in her eye. 'You mean one of those hanging up on the deck!'

'On the promenade deck,' her father added. 'Yes, that's right, they are going to lower those and you will have to go for a ride in one.'

'Will you be coming with me?' she questioned.

'No, darling,' he answered, this time choking back the tears. 'Daddy needs to stay on the ship in order to help other people. You will have to be really brave and go on your own with some other people you may not know.'

Nana saw her father's eyes glisten with tears as he spoke. She had often seen or heard him crying when praying for sinners to be saved, but she knew that this was something different.

'But, Daddy,' she said simply, 'can't I stay on the ship with you?'

'No!' her father said, with a determination in his voice. 'The ship's captain has commanded that all women and children be put into the lifeboats, so we must obey him mustn't we?'

'But I'd much rather stay with you,' she pleaded.

'Up you get,' her father coaxed, ignoring her request as he pulled her warm blankets off. 'Let's get

113

you dressed for this boat trip. You need to be nice and warm, but we must be quick. We don't want to miss your boat, do we?'

Safety for Nana

Nana was perturbed at the sudden urgency to get up and dressed. She was well aware that to go for a boat ride in the middle of the night, was not the normal thing to do. Without any more questions she climbed out of her bunk and started searching for some suitable warm clothes. There was her favourite dress which was made of thick cotton over which she pulled a knitted cardigan and her warm duffle coat. She slipped her locket into her pocket not wishing to leave the picture of her mother behind.

Her father handed her a blanket and pillow saying, 'Here, Nana, take these, they will help to keep you warm and comfy whilst you are in the boat.'

His daughter took them, reluctantly, still looking for a sign in her father's face that would mean he had changed his mind and would go with her or let her stay with him. However, all she saw was a steely determination about his every action. He reached up onto the top of the wardrobe and produced two large white life jackets. Nana stared at them wondering what they were. She had only ever seen one picture of a tortoise, but immediately the sight of these with their protruding blocks of cork, made her think of that hard-shelled animal. 'Quickly now,' her father urged. 'Put this on.'

'But why, Daddy?' his daughter protested. 'What is it?'

'A life jacket,' he answered reassuringly. 'It will help keep you afloat if you fall into the water and help to keep you warm in the boat. Hurry now, we need to put it on you.' He placed the life jacket over her head, allowing the hard ribbed shell to drop down her front and back. It was really much too big for her and came right down to her knees causing her to giggle.

'Oh, Daddy, you'd never allow me to go out dressed like this normally.'

'No, darling,' he responded, 'but this is not normally.'

Her father carried her blanket and pillow as he ushered Nana towards the cabin door. 'Daddy,' his daughter enquired, in a confused state, 'are you not going to put your life jacket on too?' She motioned towards the second life jacket her father had pulled down from the wardrobe a few moments before and was now lying unused on her bunk.

'I'll come back and pick it up later,' he answered.

'You must put it on now to help keep you warm too,' she countered with a pleading look in her eyes.

He took the life jacket and quickly placed it over his head before tying the ribbons at either side to keep it in place.

'There, are you happy now?' he enquired, as he briefly smiled down at her.

'Oh, yes,' she answered enthusiastically, 'That will keep you much warmer.'

Again, Mr Harper ushered his daughter towards the cabin door and, as he did so, he realised that the incline of the floor was becoming greater. 'Nana, quickly,' he urged, 'we must hurry.'

'Aren't you going to pray as you usually do when you are leaving me?'

Her father blushed with a tinge of guilt as he felt the impact of her words. He knew there was an urgent need to get his daughter to the lifeboats, but he also knew too that he must pray with Nana, 'Yes,' he answered simply. 'You are right child. We must pray together.'

He knelt down on the floor and pulled his daughter tightly to him as he prayed once more for the Heavenly Father's guidance, help and protection on Nana, and for wisdom for himself as he sought to help others on the ship.

Almost as soon as he had said, 'Amen,' a loud creaking sound seemed to resound around the cabin making Nana jump.

'What was that?' she asked anxiously.

'Just the ship creaking a little,' he replied, trying to keep his own fears for his daughter under control. He opened the door of the cabin and led Nana out into the passageway. Once more they moved towards the dining saloon where they had eaten so many nice meals together. Nana remembered that this was also

117

the room in which they had met and made other friends on board the ship.

Nana noticed too that they were walking downhill towards the dining area. 'Why is the floor going down?' she asked.

'I'll tell you later,' her father answered. 'Right now, we need to go up to the promenade deck.' Nearing the stairs, they came across many other passengers all making for the same place, the promenade deck where the lifeboats were and possible safety.

As they joined the crowd and began to slowly make their way up the stairs, Nana asked, 'Can we not go up in the elevator again?'

'No,' her father said firmly, 'this is the way to go.'

At the top of the staircase there stood a rather plump man complaining to a steward who was trying to assist him with his life jacket. 'This is most uncomfortable. Do we really have to wear them?'

'I am afraid so, sir,' the exasperated steward replied, as he commenced tying one side of the jacket.

'But it does not fit properly,' the man continued to moan. 'It's not wide enough.'

The steward, catching sight of Nana as she passed by, said, 'Just take a look at that little girl there. Her life belt does not fit her properly, but she isn't making any fuss.'

The plump man looked down at the little girl as his attendant fastened the other side of his life jacket. Humiliated he ceased from his complaining.

Once on the promenade deck Nana heard a man's voice calling with urgency, 'Women and children to the boats!'

John Harper deftly picked his daughter up to carry her through the crowd of people. 'Let's get you a place on this boat,' he said, trying his best to reassure the little girl.

Finally, Mr Harper managed to get close to an officer who was ushering the women and children through to a lifeboat on the port side of the ship.

'I have my daughter here for the lifeboat,' Mr Harper said, as he neared the officer. 'I'm sorry, sir,' he replied. 'This boat is full. But they are lowering the starboard lifeboats on the other side.'

'Thank you!' Mr Harper, still carrying Nana, began to make his way through the crowd to the opposite side of the ship. Nana looked back over her father's shoulder to hear the officer command, 'Stand by for lowering.' He flapped his arms and hands in order to signal to those working the winches to begin dropping the lifeboat slowly down the side of the ship. Nana giggled as she looked at his arms flapping widely as the lifeboat dropped down out of sight.

'What's so funny?' asked her father, as he tried to make headway across the deck.

'I was just watching that man flapping his arms. He looked like he was trying to fly,' she laughed.

Eventually with many, 'Excuse me's,' and, 'I have a child for the boats,' Nana's father managed to push his way across to the starboard side of the ship. Here, too, the crew had made a ring around the boats and were only allowing women and children to enter, although there did appear to be one or two men sitting in them!

'Is there room for my daughter?' he enquired earnestly.

'Do we have room for a little girl?' an officer enquired.

'No, we are full already,' a harsh voice resounded from the boat.

'We can take her,' a kind lady's voice sounded from inside another lifeboat.

'Right, young lady,' the officer said as he gently lifted Nana from her father and walked with her over towards the boat.

'Take care, Nana,' her father called, as he waved to her from behind the cordon of crewmen who were restricting access to the lifeboat. 'I love you!'

He could just make out his daughter mouthing the words, 'I love you too, Daddy,' as she was being handed over and placed into the lifeboat. He stood and watched as the officer stood on the deck and called, 'That's all for this boat.' Turning to the crewmen manning the winch gear, the officer called out, 'Prepare to lower!'

Other people were standing on either side of Mr Harper, all waving and saying goodbye to their relatives and friends. Nana and her father continued to wave to each other until the boat disappeared down the *Titanic's* side and out of sight. Only then did Nana's father pull out his handkerchief and wipe his tear-stained face and moist eyes.

'You have managed to get Nana away in a boat,' a voice sounded behind him. Mr Harper turned to see Eva's father standing looking at him with a blank expression on his face. 'My two have just left in Boat 14,' he said. 'At least they will be safe.'

'Good,' Mr Harper replied, still wiping his eyes, 'Nana's just left in Boat 11.'

'What do you think will happen to the rest of us?' Mr Harrison enquired hoarsely. 'What if a rescue ship doesn't arrive in time?'

'I cannot think of anything that a man or woman left on this ship needs more than God's great salvation,' the faithful preacher replied.

Mr Harrison looked at him seriously. 'Do you really think that God will forgive and save at the eleventh hour?' he asked.

'Yes. He most certainly will. The blood of the Lord Jesus can make anyone clean and ready for heaven if they are just prepared to repent and believe.'

'But how do I know what you are telling me is true?' Mr Harrison asked. 'I need to think about this.'

'Just don't leave it too long,' Mr Harper replied. 'The Bible clearly says that "Now is the accepted time, now is the day of salvation".'

A sudden surge of passengers rushed down the deck, parting the two men as mass panic broke out among those remaining on the ship. Many were pushing aimlessly through the large number of people who were standing around. Suddenly, a rocket shot up from the ship with a sharp crack followed by a screaming fizzing sound as it climbed high into the air from the port side of the ship. It exploded in a hail of brilliant white stars that lit up the darkness of the night sky. The noise of this, followed by the brilliant but short-lived flash of white light, brought a sudden hushed silence to everyone on the decks of the great ship. Hope suddenly rang in everyone's heart. Surely a ship would see the rockets as they burst high in the sky. Surely some nearby ship would respond to the emergency SOS messages that were being relayed from the *Titanic's* wireless room. Surely help and rescue would come in time to save them.

The Repentant Thief

Mr Harper hurried back to his cabin. It took some effort to push his way through the seething mass of humanity that was still making its way up from below decks to the lifeboats. The main staircase was alive with people all pushing and shoving each other as they tried to get up into the coldness of the night air. Eventually, he managed to get back down to the saloon deck level where his cabin was located. As he walked along the main corridor, he noticed that he was walking uphill at a much steeper angle than when he had made this journey to collect his daughter. Not only was the angle decidedly steeper, but there was also a list to the starboard side which made keeping balance and walking in the middle of the corridor hard work. Quickly, he opened the cabin door and went inside. There, on the dressing table, was his little New Testament. Picking it up, he placed it carefully into his coat pocket and hurried back out, leaving his suitcase, clothes, wallet and other possessions in the cabin.

As he retraced his steps towards the dining saloon he caught sight of a mother struggling with her own little girl down one of the smaller corridors that led to the cabins.

'Here,' he said offering his hand, 'Let me help you.'

The lady spoke a language that Mr Harper did not understand. However, she realised that he wanted to help. Taking the lady by the hand he guided her quickly towards the foot of the stairs leading up to the lifeboats. The stairway was still crowded. He took the little girl in his arms and called out, 'Make way for women and children.' Surprisingly, most of the crowd moved back, leaving a small gap between them which allowed Mr Harper to pass with the child and the mother close behind. All the time he called out, 'Make way for women and children, please.' When he reached the promenade deck he was relieved to see a crewman standing just in front of him. 'Which way to the boats?' he enquired earnestly.

'Over on the port side, sir,' the man answered. 'But you'll have to be quick they are filling fast now.'

'Thank you.' Mr Harper moved past the man and on towards where he now knew the lifeboats were still being filled. Pushing his way through the people he continued to cry, 'Women and children here for the boats! Make way, please!'

Eventually he made it to the officer who was supervising the loading of the boats. 'I have a little girl here and a lady for the boats,' he said in a relieved manner. 'Through here,' the officer said curtly, as he ushered the preacher through the cordon. Mr Harper carefully set the little girl down on the ground and turning to her mother said, 'There you are, ma'am. The Lord bless you.'

The lady turned and with tear-stained eyes, took the pastor's hand and shook it vigorously. Then she said in stuttering, broken English, 'I ... thank ...you!'

The two crewmen handed the little girl between themselves into the boat and helped the mother to follow.

'Excuse me,' an urgent voice sounded from behind him. 'Can I speak to you, please, sir?' Mr Harper turned to see the young man who had stolen his New Testament. 'I have been thinking carefully about what you were telling me, about heaven and hell, forgiveness of sin and trusting in the Lord Jesus.' The man's eyes were filled with emotion. 'I figure that I haven't got long to live now, so I need to know I am right for heaven! Will you show me the way?' he begged.

'Of course I will,' the preacher answered kindly. 'It's amazing that you found me in this crowd.'

'I must be honest,' the young man replied, 'I told God that if he was real I would see you again and just a short time after, you passed by me on the stairs so I followed you here.'

'That's great,' Mr Harper replied. 'Let's go away from this crowd so we can speak more easily.'

They headed in the direction of the dining saloon. There were not so many people pushing up the staircase now and Mr Harper and the young man were able to walk down it relatively easily. One deck down and Mr Harper pointed to the library. 'Let's go in here,' he suggested.

Once inside the large ornate room, with its various shelves of books, the two men sat down. The ever-steepening incline of the ship made sitting comfortably a little difficult. Mr Harper took out his New Testament and looking the man in the eye asked, 'Are you afraid to die tonight?'

The young man looked up at him with a startled expression upon his face and answered, 'Yes! Yes, I am! I am terrified!'

'That's good,' the preacher replied, with a solemn note to his voice. 'But before we go any further I would love to know your name?'

'John,' the man answered, 'John Flynn from County Tipperary.'

Mr Harper looked at him, 'I am a John as well,' he answered kindly, 'and a man called John wrote in this book the words, "Let not your heart be troubled". You see, John, when someone trusts the Lord Jesus as their Saviour and repents of their sins, they have no need to be troubled or frightened about anything, even death. The Lord Jesus will give us his peace so that we can face whatever may come our way. Tonight, as this ship is sinking, I have perfect peace with God because I have Jesus Christ as my Saviour and Lord. Therefore, I have no fears about dying. I am sad, very sad that I may never see my little girl again, but I know that the Lord will not let her down or fail her, if he chooses to take me to heaven.'

'I wish I had that kind of peace and assurance,' John answered, 'but I am afraid I have been so bad that God will never ever be able to forgive me.'

'But he can!' Mr Harper responded quickly. 'Listen to these words of the Lord Jesus that John has written for us, "For God so loved the world that he gave his only begotten Son that whosoever believeth in him should not perish but have everlasting life". This message is for the whosoever. You could write your own name in there. It does not matter how bad you are. Trust him and believe that when he died, he died to take your punishment and provide for you a place in heaven. God loves you so very much.'

The young man looked up into Mr Harper's face as recognition lit up his face and lifted his gloom. 'I see now,' he said. 'God loves me despite my sin.'

'Yes,' answered Mr Harper enthusiastically.

'And because of his love, he is willing to forgive my past and make me fit for heaven tonight, even so close to dying.'

'That's right, he is.'

'Then tonight I will take him as my Saviour.' The young man was almost radiant with joy and happiness as he bowed his head and repented of his sin, trusting in the one who had died for him on the cross. After a couple of minutes he looked up. 'There, I have trusted him! He's my Saviour! I am now ready to die.'

'Praise the Lord!' echoed the preacher with a smile. 'Now, the Lord expects you to tell others about him. He wants you to let others know that he can save them too.'

'I will, Mr Harper, I will right now.' With that he rose from his chair and walked towards the library door across the rapidly tilting floor. As he reached it, the door opened and an older man carrying a stick walked in.

Mr Flynn wasted no time in saying, 'Excuse me. Did you know that God's Son, the Lord Jesus, died for you and can make you fit for heaven?'

The man stopped and looked at the young man in a surprised manner. 'I beg your pardon.'

'I said, did you know that the Lord Jesus can make you fit for heaven?' Mr Flynn repeated, 'and with this ship sinking as it is, you need a Saviour tonight.'

The man grunted and said, 'I don't intend to die tonight. I fully intend to get into a lifeboat.' With that he turned and walked back out again.

John Flynn shrugged his shoulders at Mr Harper who had been listening in delight. 'That was a good effort,' Mr Harper said encouragingly. 'Keep trying.' The young, saved, thief made his way out of the library and up the stairs to find his friends to tell them too.

Unbelievers to the Lifeboats

It was all quiet in the library and Mr Harper sat in the silence, broken only by the creaking and groaning of the ship. Occasionally, an ornament slipped off a table or some books fell from the shelves onto the floor. Mr Harper bowed his head in silent prayer once again, as he thanked God for allowing Nana to get away in a lifeboat and also for saving the young man. He now prayed for strength and help to show others their need of the Lord Jesus, before the ship sank and all hope was gone.

Mr Harper made his way back to the deck where so many people were still flocking. 'Pastor!' Pastor!' a voice called from among the countless people. Mr Harper looked into the mob trying to see where the voice had come from. 'Pastor!' It echoed again and suddenly he caught sight of one of the officers waving at him frantically as he tried to push his way through the people towards him.

'Pastor, would you please help us get the women and children into the lifeboats?' the young man said, with a note of urgency in his voice. 'It seems that so many do not fully realise the danger the ship is in and will not get into the boats. I thought, seeing you were a pastor, they might listen to you.'

Mr Harper hesitated as he looked at the young man in the smart officer's uniform and cap of the White Star line. 'I don't know why they should listen to me any more than you, but I'll certainly do what I can. Which boats are being launched now?'

The officer pointed down the side of the ship to where he could just see two lifeboats waiting in their davits to be lowered, but which so far had very few takers for the number of seats available. 'Those,' he answered simply before adding, 'Thank you.'

Using all the power of his voice to cut through the night air, the preacher called out clearly above the hubbub of the crowd, 'Women, children and unbelievers to the lifeboats quickly, please.' He moved through them, continually calling the same urgent message, 'Women, children and unbelievers to the lifeboats, please.'

One man stopped him. 'What do you mean by unbelievers, man?' he asked sharply.

'Those who are not going to heaven,' Mr Harper responded. 'You need Christ as your Saviour to be ready to die. If he is not your Saviour, you need to get into a lifeboat quickly.'

A man was standing nearby talking to his wife, 'You know, dear, I think that man is right. We need to be ready to meet God and at the moment we're not.'

On and on he walked across the barrier that had separated first and second class and towards the bow of the ship that was now almost awash with the cold green water of the Atlantic Ocean. This view of the ship dipping so gently, yet so certainly towards her death made him redouble his efforts. 'Women, children and unbelievers into the lifeboats, please. There is not much time.'

As he walked back up the sloping deck of the ship, he found a family, almost frozen with fear, holding onto the bottom of a large wire rope that supported the base of one of the great funnels. 'Will you help me, please?' the man asked. 'My family do not want to leave me.'

'I have already put my daughter off in a lifeboat,' the preacher answered, 'and you're right. You need to do the same.'

'But my little girl does not have a life jacket,' the mother cried in alarm.

Mr Harper quickly undid his own life jacket and, lifting it off his head, placed it over the little girl tying it tightly around her. As he stood up, he noticed the way the jacket hung down to the girl's knees like Nana's had and he thought of how Nana had insisted he put his on to keep him warm. 'There,' he said, 'now she has a life jacket and I think you should obey your husband and get into a lifeboat. There is not a moment to lose.'

Quickly, he helped lift the lady up from where she was sitting and guided her towards the lifeboats that were being filled. The husband followed behind with his two children. He led them through the crew cordon to the lifeboat that assured safety for the mother and her daughters. Without being able to fully say goodbye, the lady and the girls were ushered by the crew into the lifeboat. Once they were seated, they turned with fearful faces to wave to their bewildered father and husband who was left standing next to Mr Harper.

From her own crowded lifeboat, and seated among people she did not know, little Nana watched as two men pulled hard at the oars to row the lifeboat away from the sinking ship. As she looked around at the huddled occupants of the boat, she noticed many of the ladies were dressed in mink coats and fur scarves, others wore large brightly coloured hats. She looked at her own duffle coat underneath her life jacket. It felt drab and shabby against the splendour of the outfits some of the ladies were wearing. However, against the chill of the cold night air, she was thankful for it and the blanket, too, which she held tight around her shoulders. She turned back to gaze at the huge ship. Its dark form was silhouetted in the night sky. Hundreds of lights were still shining through the portholes and along the various open decks. The sea around the ship had an eerie glow as lights reflected in the glass-like calm of the water. High above, she saw a multitude of stars shining down upon the scene, their brilliant white rays lighting up the darkness of the clear sky. She listened to the water which gently lapped around the lifeboat. The oars splashed as the boat made its slow progress away from the danger of the huge ship.

Nana noticed that the *Titanic* was now at an angle to the sea, with the bows completely under water. Many, looking at the sight from the safety of the small boat, were crying as they thought of loved ones left behind.

Nana was only six and did not fully comprehend the great danger her father was in. Although she could see the ship was progressively sinking at the bows, the fact that it was in danger of disappearing altogether, had not fully dawned upon her young mind. 'Right then,' one of the rowers said in a tired sort of voice, 'that's far enough!'

'Oi,' answered a man in a dirty boiler suit, who was holding the tiller, 'I'm in charge here, not you and I say keep rowing!'

'But we are far enough away now, aren't we?' the man with the oars answered.

'Not for my liking,' replied the grubby man. 'When that ship goes down it will cause a huge amount of suction and drag us down with it, if we're too close. Now, row harder.'

A large American lady was sitting next to Nana and turning to her asked, 'Is your mother not with you?'

'No,' Nana replied, still staring across the calm water to the foundering ship, 'my mummy's in heaven and my daddy's still on the *Titanic*.'

'Oh, my dear,' the lady said, putting her arm around the little girl and pulling her close to her. 'You poor thing.'

Nearer my God to Thee

Back on board the ship, many were getting desperate as it became more and more apparent that the ship the world thought to be unsinkable, was going to go down. It was clear there was not going to be enough room for everyone on the lifeboats. Men and women were hugging each other and frantically saying goodbye. The crew were struggling to keep control as they tried to fill the two remaining boats. Mr Harper heard someone shout, 'Don't panic!' which was followed by a mass surge of bodies towards the boats. Suddenly, three shots rang out in quick succession, piercing the night air and bringing a sudden hush to the thronging people.

'Don't panic!' an officer cried again through the quiet that had descended. 'Please, keep calm.'

The silence lasted only for a few seconds before the terror took hold. People, realising that there was unlikely to be any more room in the lifeboats, moved en masse towards the stern of the great liner.

Mr Harper walked about trying to give what little help and comfort he could to those who were calm enough to listen.

In the distance he could hear the jaunty strains of the ship's orchestra as they were playing happy up-tempo numbers at the top of the staircase he had so often used with Nana. For a moment the music stopped and only the desperate clamour and calls of passengers could be heard. Then suddenly, slowly, mournfully the strain of a single violin penetrated the noise and hushed the cries of the frantic people. A few bars into the tune and the other musical instruments joined in. Mr Harper distinctly recognised the tune:

'Nearer my God to Thee, Nearer to Thee
E'en though it be a cross that raiseth me
Still all my song would be nearer my God to Thee
Nearer my God to Thee, Nearer to Thee.'

'How near are the men and women that are still stranded on this mighty vessel to meeting God?' Mr Harper thought as he listened to the slow sad tune. Some, who could recall the words from memory, joined in the strain of the simple melody.

'There let the way appear steps unto heaven
All that Thou sendest me in mercy given
Angels to beckon me nearer my God to Thee
Nearer my God to thee, nearer to thee!'

The sound of the music died, to again be replaced by the clamour of passengers making their way towards the stern of the ship.

As he walked up the rapidly-steepening decks, an older gentleman stopped him. 'Are you the preacher who was with his little girl at the hymn singing service earlier this evening?'

'Yes, I am,' he replied courteously. 'Why do you ask?'

'Well, the ship is sinking. I see that all the lifeboats are almost gone and I guess the sea is freezing, so I need to be ready to die. I thought you might be able to help me to put things right with God, so I'll be ready for heaven.'

'My dear fellow, I would be delighted to tell you how to be ready for heaven.'

'I have never been worried about my life or the thought of dying before, but now I know I must be ready to meet God,' the man continued.

'Then you need to trust the Lord Jesus Christ, God's Son as your Saviour. He died on a cross to take your sins away, was buried and rose again to be your Saviour and secure a place in heaven for you. Are you willing to trust him?'

'Yes, I am but,' the man paused uneasily, 'is he willing to receive someone who only wants to be saved because he is so close to death?'

'He saved the thief dying next to him on a cross, so he is willing to save you, if you are willing to trust him,' Mr Harper explained. 'The Bible says, "Believe on the Lord Jesus Christ and thou shalt be saved".'

Just then the *Titanic* took a sudden and unexpected dip, as more water rushed in through its buckled side. The various bulkheads in the bottom of the ship gave way, allowing huge quantities of water to flood into more parts of the liner. This unexpected surge caused both men to lose their footing and fall onto the wooden deck. The man with whom Mr Harper had been speaking, slipped down the deck towards the bow of the ship. Mr Harper had managed to grab hold of a wooden bench to stop himself from going the same way. The three huge propellers had now been hoisted clear of the water by the downward pull of the bow section of the ship. This made any form of walking on the ship not only difficult, but very hazardous as people and items slid down the decks like children on a giant slide. Carefully, Mr Harper climbed to his feet, watching several wooden deck chairs slip past him towards the sea. With difficulty, he managed to hold tight to the metal railings that ran along the inside of the deck and he slowly made his way back towards the rapidly lifting stern. Stopping, he looked back just in time to see an upturned lifeboat float off from the roof of the officers' quarters. In the water, he could see people swimming towards this means of safety.

His mind went to his own daughter somewhere out on that ocean, safe in a little lifeboat. He looked up to heaven and committed her to the Lord asking that God, his Heavenly Father, would keep her safe and bring her up in a way that would bring honour to him.

As he saw the water rising rapidly up the deck towards him, he knew that to stay on board the ship would be folly. He watched as numerous people jumped or dived off the decks into the freezing sea below. Many of them were knocked out as they hit the water, their life jackets with their hard exterior jarring their chin and necks as a result of jumping from such a height.

Mr Harper decided to carefully cross the deck as best he could and hold onto the rails along the side of the ship. His plan was to carefully slip off as the water reached him and then swim away as quickly as possible. Once safely across the deck, he watched as the bridge of the ship plunged into the green, icy depths. A man above him was throwing wooden deck chairs into the sea in the hope that some might be able to use them as floats. Another person slid past, trying desperately to hold onto a sort of raft that he had made.

Suddenly he heard a loud 'crack'. Initially, he thought it was another shot from an officer's gun, reverberating somewhere below him. Then came a second 'crack,' followed by another and another in quick succession. He still thought someone must be firing a gun in order to keep control, but then he caught sight of a rope, a gigantic metal rope, flailing up high into the air as further cracks echoed across the still, dark night. Transfixed, he watched in horror as the forward funnel broke free from its position, ever so slowly at first and then faster and faster as its guy ropes snapped under the enormous strain. It crashed down into the sea above where the bows were submerged. Sparks flew all around and a large cloud of soot and steam rose into the air from its ruptured base. There were people swimming below where it was falling. Mr Harper called out at the top of his voice, 'Look out!' but his frantic warning was drowned out by the noise of the ripping steel and snapping ropes. No sooner had the funnel hit the water than it was gone, sinking like a stone into the dark depths of the Atlantic Ocean.

Mr Harper could hear the awful cries of many voices as they struggled to keep alive in the freezing water. He longed to help them. How he longed to preach to them as a dying man to dying men. He called out into the night as loudly as he could, 'Jesus says, "Come unto me all ye that labour and are heavy laden and I will give you rest".'

'Maybe some poor struggling soul will hear,' he thought.

Just then there was a rumble and a groan from down inside the hull of the ship, such as he had never heard before all night. It was a deep cavernous noise that made his hair stand on end. He had got used to the creaking of the ship as it had been making such noises for nearly two hours, but this thunderous sound was different. Not only was it exceedingly loud, but it sent a sharp vibration throughout the ship causing many holding on to railings, seats and other items to lose their grip and fall from their places of refuge. Many of the women still on board screamed at the noise and resulting motion of the vessel. Then suddenly and without warning the lights flickered for a second and went out completely causing total darkness to descend upon the scene.

Mr Harper's eyes slowly adjusted to the dim light the starlit skies provided. However, far worse than the dark was the sound of human voices all crying in fear and terror as they realised that the end of the mighty *Titanic* was only seconds away. A verse of a hymn that he had known from childhood came flooding into John Harper's mind.

> 'Let the lower lights be burning
> Send their beam across the wave
> Some poor struggling fainting seaman
> You may rescue, you may save.'

Here was his encouragement. Here in the middle of the night, in the middle of the Atlantic Ocean during what, no doubt, would be the greatest disaster of his time, he must continue to point men and women to the light of the world, the Lord Jesus Christ.

The water which continued to rapidly claim the once elegant and majestic ship looked inky-black as it rose up the timber decking towards where Mr Harper hung onto the ship's railings. His mind raced back several years to another occasion when he felt sure he was going to drown and he remembered the great calm that had descended upon him at that time. The Lord would see him through, he was sure of that. He thought again of Nana safe in Lifeboat 11. How would she manage without a father or a mother to look after, care for and guide her? Suddenly, his feet went icy cold and looking down he realised that the rising water had now reached him. He let the icy waters rise up his legs to his calves and knees before he took a deep breath and jumped into the freezing cold sea.

Home to Heaven

From the crowded lifeboat, now safely out of danger from the suction of the sinking vessel, Nana continued to look on in bewilderment as the stern of the *Titanic* lifted higher and higher out of the water. She was mesmerised by the strange glow that she could see as the lights on the inside of the ship still shone out through the submerged porthole windows. Her thoughts went to her friend, Eva. Was she safe? Had she also been put into a lifeboat without her daddy? What about Charlie? Would this be to him just another of his adventures? Oh, how she wanted both her daddy and new friends to be with her. Suddenly a lady's voice sounded anxiously from behind her, 'Look! Look!'

Everyone turning in the direction of the giant ship heard the most thunderous noise echo across the barren night. Huge bangs and crashes rang out from the ship as boilers left their beds and fell unstoppable towards the submerged bows of the ship. The angle of the ship had become so steep that anything that was not secured was falling forward causing smaller smashing noises to be heard across the sea. Then without warning the lights on the great ship flickered off, came on again for about a second, and then went out for ever. There was a stunned silence as those in the safety of the lifeboat took in the awful sight that unfolded before them. The great unsinkable *Titanic,* the pride of man's final victory over the seas, lay stricken before them, a black silhouette in front of a dark sky as it fought its hopeless battle to stay afloat. After the initial silence in the lifeboat, a lady began to scream hysterically. Another wept uncontrollably and others turned away from the sight of the great ship with its stern rising ever higher into the air. Nana, frightened, was completely unaware of the great battle her father was about to have for his own life and the souls of his fellow passengers in the frigid waters of the North Atlantic.

As Mr Harper jumped from the side of the *Titanic* he felt the deck slide away from under his feet. The intense cold took his breath away and felt like a thousand knives cutting deep into his body. Initially, he stopped breathing with the shock of entering the water. Then summoning all the strength he could muster he began to swim clear of the floundering ship. The intense cold made any physical work hard and he had only swum about ten metres when he began to feel totally exhausted. He was thankful to see a deck chair floating on the surface of the water. Upon reaching it, he took hold of it with both hands and allowed himself to rest. He was breathing fast as a result of the cold and was beginning to shiver violently. He turned to look back at the *Titanic* as it stood almost vertically behind him, like some giant black finger pointing high into the sky. The sea was now alive with people throwing themselves off the ship. The *Titanic's* battle to stay afloat would soon be over. As he looked all around, he wondered just how he could help so many people who were, like him, so close to eternity. What could he say or do to offer comfort and help to the dying on every side? Then suddenly the Holy Spirit brought a passage of scripture from Isaiah to his still clear and active mind. He lifted up his voice and called out into the night.

'Look unto me, and be ye saved, all the ends of the earth: for I am God, and there is none else.'

The cold was numbing and Mr Harper had difficulty in raising his voice to the level he would have liked for people to hear. However, almost as soon as he had said it, a man swam across to him with a life ring under one arm. The preacher recognised him, despite the dark and the commotion all around, as the man he had seen as the ship had taken its sudden surge into the water. 'It looks like she's going,' the man said, as he nodded in the direction of the *Titanic* as it slowly sank down into the water behind them.

'There's no hope for the ship,' Mr Harper responded, 'but there is for you! Are you saved yet?'

'No. N...N...No,' the man shivered in answer.

'Then believe on the Lord Jesus Christ and thou shalt be saved,' the preacher retorted with urgency.

'But how?' the man answered hoarsely. Then he added, 'Look, we ought to get clear of the ship or the suction will drag us down.'

Both men started to swim further away from the ship's side. It was a real effort, but they managed to get far enough away and then turned to watch its final sad moments. It slid down, down, down slowly then suddenly quicker as if some unseen hand hidden below the water was dragging it down with great and inescapable force. The last remaining funnel disappeared below the waterline, then the waters rushed around the stern, cranes and gantry before finally with hardly a sound, she was gone, leaving just a frothy gurgling cauldron of bubbles to show where she had been.

There was a moment of quiet from those struggling in the water as, spellbound, they watched her go.

Mr Harper, still holding onto his deck chair for support, could feel the cold biting into his bones. His head felt light and he knew that in the terrible cold of the sea, his life on earth would soon be gone. He wanted to shout out verses of help and encouragement from the Bible, but even drawing breath was hard as the water numbed his body. The man close by, again, turned to the preacher and in a voice just loud enough to hear asked, 'How can I be ready for heaven?'

'Just believe and you will be saved,' Mr Harper repeated desperately, unaware at how weak his voice sounded.

'I will! I will!' the man cried out. 'I need God's forgiveness, I really do.'

Mr Harper waited, shivering, trying his hardest to keep conscious as the numbness of the biting cold gradually crept over his body. Concentration was hard as he felt a fog come in and cloud his thinking.

Then, with renewed strength in his voice, the man cried, 'I've taken Christ as my Saviour and am ready for heaven. Oh, how wonderful is God's love that even now he will receive a sinner such as me.'

'P...P...Praise...the...L...L...Lord,' Mr Harper stammered through his violently chattering teeth. He then closed his eyes as a wonderful peace flooded into his mind and he caught a vision of heavenly glory. In a whisper he said, 'Lord Jesus ... receive my spirit ... and take good care of Nana for me ... I'm ... coming ... home ... to heaven.'

The man watched as an angelic smile spread over the preacher's face. He heard the slow stammering prayer to God and then saw Mr Harper deliberately let go of his deck chair and his limp body vanished from sight into the cold black sea below.

Instantly, the man knew that he must survive in order to tell John Harper's story.[1] Kept afloat only by his life belt, he started swimming from where the *Titanic* had vanished, towards what he thought must be a small group of lifeboats. The large and cumbersome

---

[1] John Harper's last convert remains unnamed. Although records exist of his eye-witness testimony, his identity has been lost through time.

life belt made swimming harder, but he knew that to abandon it would result in certain death. To his great joy he saw a lifeboat making towards him. A man standing upright was shining a torch from side to side across the water. He stopped swimming and tried to call, but all that came out was a husky croak. He tried again 'He…lp! He…re!' But it was no use. He was totally unable to raise his voice louder than a whisper. He raised his arms as high as he could and splashed around. As the boat drew close, the man with the torch heard the splashes and noticed the movement. Shining his light in the direction of the noise, the penetrating beam of the torch picked out the survivor.

'Port helm,' the man with the torch cried. The men rowing turned the boat ever so slowly to the left, in the direction of where the man was struggling in the water. Carefully, they lowered him gently onto the floor of the boat. He looked up into the face of his rescuers and before slipping into unconsciousness, smiled weakly, saying, 'Thank you.'

Those in Nana's lifeboat grew silent as they witnessed the awful sight of the *Titanic's* last minutes. Shock and horror fell upon each one as suddenly she was gone. There were people crying out at the pain of knowing they had probably lost a husband or father. But for the most part, those on board the little overcrowded boat sat in numbed silence. Nana sat stunned. She had seen the great ship go down, but in her heart she hoped somewhere her daddy was safe.

Slowly, the long night drew on and some of the crew members sought to gather the many lifeboats together, to make rescue easier when other ships arrived. The kind American lady's arm stayed firmly round Nana, while Nana shared her blanket to help keep them both warm.

Suddenly, in the distance a white rocket shot up high into the night sky before breaking into a shower of small stars.

'A rescue boat!' someone called out.

'The *Carpathia*!' another shouted. 'It must be.'

A couple of minutes later, just as the sky was beginning to lighten in the east with the promise of a new day, another rocket went up into the sky. Rescue was close. Half an hour later, the clear silhouette of a ship came into sight on the horizon, with its green and red lights shining brightly. It seemed that the rescue ship was stationary for a long time until the people in Nana's lifeboat realised that it had stopped to pick up passengers from lifeboats that had travelled further from the scene of the *Titanic's* sinking. It was another two hours before the ship slowly and carefully pulled up along side the lifeboat containing little Nana. As it came closer, Nana noticed that the rescue ship was large, but not nearly as large as the *Titanic* had been. It had one big funnel set in the centre of its length and it appeared to have no covering on its bridge to protect the crew who controlled the ship. As the ship neared the little lifeboat, Nana started to spell out the ship's name as its large bows passed alongside her lifeboat. '*Car...path....i...a,*' she said slowly.

'Yes, this is the *Carpathia* dear.' A lady sitting close by, turned to see Nana staring up at the side of the ship. 'It's such a tragedy that it could not have been here sooner to rescue everybody!'

The large doors along the side of the ship were open and rope ladders were slung down the sides. Most of the passengers were able to climb up. Nana was glad that her father had insisted she wear warm clothing. She was also glad he had given her the blanket. With a little help, she took her turn to climb the precarious rope ladder up through one of the open doors on the ship's side. Here, a man was writing down the names of the passengers as they entered the ship.

'What's your name?' he asked Nana kindly.

Suddenly the little girl went very shy, realising that her father was not around to help her, or answer for her. She looked at the man in a puzzled manner as he again calmly asked her name.

'Nana,' she said simply, without expression.

'Nana who,' he enquired further.

'Nana Harper,' she replied again, with little enthusiasm.

'Thank you,' the man said, smiling at her.

'This way, please, young miss,' another man said, beckoning her towards him with his hand. In a daze,

Nana walked further into the ship before she was taken into another large room. Here, many of the survivors, who had already boarded the rescue ship, were sitting sipping soup and hot drinks. Nana felt isolated and lonely without her father. She looked frantically for him, surveying each face in the room. She was worried that he would be anxiously searching for her and longed to tell him that she was alright. As she looked through some glass-panelled doors she saw Eva's mother talking to a member of the crew. She ran to the doors and pushed them open calling, 'Mrs Harrison, is Eva here?'

Before Mrs Harrison could answer, a call came across the room, 'Nana!'

Nana turned to see Eva running towards her. The two girls threw their arms around each other.

'Have you seen my daddy?' Nana asked her friend.

'No, and I haven't seen mine either,' Eva said solemnly.

'I'm sure that they will be here somewhere,' Nana answered optimistically.

Eva looked at her younger companion, whilst trying to hold back her tears. 'Mummy says there wasn't enough room in the lifeboats for everyone, so Daddy will not have been able to get into one.'

Nana looked at her friend with a puzzled expression. 'What do you mean?' she quizzed.

'Well, there were too many people on the ship and not enough lifeboats for everyone, so some were left behind on the *Titanic,* like my daddy.' Eva could contain herself no longer. 'Oh, Nana I think my daddy's dead.'

Just at that moment Eva's mother returned and, in her despair, she placed her arms round Eva. Her face crumpled into a picture of sadness as she sobbed. 'They have picked up all the lifeboats, but Daddy was not on any of them.'

'Was my daddy on any of them?' Nana asked hopefully.

Mrs Harrison looked up from holding her daughter, then, as if seeing Nana for the first time, she cried, 'Oh, my little darling,' and pulled her into an embrace. Trying desperately to pull herself together, Mrs Harrison went to make more enquiries.

Eva called as she left, 'Please, ask about Charlie too!'

Orphaned

It did not take Eva's mother long to ascertain that neither Mr Harper nor young, cheeky Charlie Applewhite had come on board the *Carpathia* from any of the lifeboats that had been picked up.

'Daddy will be alright,' Nana enthused. 'I made him put on his life belt.' Then, breaking into a smile, she added, 'It fitted him much better than me!'

'Oh, dear child,' Mrs Harrison said, as she pulled both girls close to her, 'the water is so very cold...' Her voice trailed away as she realised that, whereas Eva still had a mother, as far as she knew, Nana had no one.

The days passed very slowly on the *Carpathia,* as it took them on their final part of the journey to America. The ship was dreadfully overcrowded as the crew sought to contend, not only with their own passengers, but also an extra seven hundred they had rescued from the *Titanic's* lifeboats.

There were countless questions to be asked as to how this huge tragedy could possibly have occurred. Why had there not been enough lifeboats for everyone on board? Many were seeking explanations from any of the surviving crew of the *Titanic* whom they happened to find. Some tried to speak to Mr Bruce

Ismay, the Chairman of the White Star Line, who had managed to find himself a place on one of the lifeboats. Mr Ismay was keeping himself well away, locked in his own cabin, emerging only to send a wireless message to either his company or the authorities waiting for them in New York.

Initially, the ship zigzagged back and forth across the area in which the *Titanic* had sunk, occasionally stopping and lowering a lifeboat in order to pick up some dead body that had been spotted floating in the icy waters. Those hardy passengers that ventured out on deck and looked over the ship's side, could see debris from the sunken ship as they floated past: deck chairs, life belts, empty life jackets, broken pieces of wood, children's toys.

Far below, and out of sight in the dark, cold murky depths of the mighty Atlantic Ocean, lay the broken wreck of what had been claimed to be the 'unsinkable' ship of dreams and it had taken with it one thousand, five hundred lives.

Nana was comforted by Mrs Harrison and others who discovered that she was now, not only motherless, but fatherless as well. As the days passed, Nana still kept hoping and praying that she would see her father's bright smile and hear his familiar voice as he came in through some door of the ship. But her dreams of such a happy reunion would never really happen. It took time for Nana to come to terms with the fact that her father had gone to heaven, but she comforted herself that he would be happy there, seeing his Saviour and meeting her own mother once again. She hoped that he had not suffered much in the last minutes of his life and that he had been comforted to know that she was safe and well.

But what had happened to Charlie, she wondered? Had he been unable to leave his father's side, or with his carefree attitude had he just left it too late to go up on deck? She had seen Mrs Smithers on the *Carpathia* so knew that she was safe, but what about the others she had made friends with? Had Mr and Mrs Collings been taken to heaven too? What about Mr Astor who had so kindly brought her and her friends those large bags of candy? Had he died? She had heard that his wife was safe. She wondered if her father managed to speak to him again of the riches of heaven, as the *Titanic* plunged to the bottom of the sea.

What would happen to her now that both her parents had died? So many things raced through her young mind in the hours that slowly passed, as she waited to arrive in New York. She took out her locket that had been in her coat pocket and opened it, lovingly. Once again she gazed at the only picture of her mother that she had. She knew she had to get a picture of her father to go alongside it. She comforted herself with a verse from the Bible her father had taught her: 'All things work together for good to them that love God to them that are called according to his purpose.' Yes, perhaps God had called them to go on the *Titanic* so that her father could speak to those he may never have otherwise been able to speak to, about the Lord Jesus. There was the pickpocket and Mr Astor, the millionaire; Mrs Smithers, the banker's wife and maybe others she would never know about. She would just have to trust in the wisdom and knowledge of God, knowing that he would never leave her or forsake her, as she now faced an uncertain future alone without father or mother.

John Harper – who was he?

John Harper was born on 29th May, 1872 in Houston, Renfrewshire, Scotland to Christian parents. When he was thirteen years old, on Sunday, 28th March, 1886, young John realised his need of the Lord Jesus as his Saviour and repented of his sins, trusting him through the words of John Chapter 3 verse 16: 'For God so loved the world that he gave his only begotten Son, that whosoever believeth in him should not perish, but have everlasting life'.

At seventeen years of age, John began to preach in the open air around his native Bridge of Weir, some six miles west of Glasgow. After nearly six years of working in a local mill by day and preaching the gospel, each evening, in 1890, John was called by God into full-time service. He moved to the Glasgow district of Govan and began to preach among the tenement buildings in that area. A few years later he went to preach at the Paisley Road Baptist Church. Ten years after his death, the Church moved to Craigiehall Street (where it still continues to function) being renamed as the 'Harper Memorial Church'. The church started with twenty-five members, but when John left to take up a position in London during September 1910, the congregation numbered in excess of five hundred!

Around the year 1903, John married Miss Annie Bell, also from Bridge of Weir, and on 1st January

1906, Jessica Annie was born. Sadly, it was just a few days after Nana's birth that her mother passed away, leaving John to look after Nana without his wife's help.

In 1910, John was approached and asked to take up the pastorate at Walworth Road Baptist Church in London. It was from here that he was asked to travel to Chicago for three months at the close of 1911, in order to preach in the Moody church there (named after famed American Evangelist Dwight L. Moody). His three months of meetings were used in a mighty way by God and John Harper was asked to return again in 1912. It was on this trip with his daughter, Nana, and niece, Miss Jessie W Leitch, that the *Titanic* hit the iceberg and foundered. Miss Leitch and Nana were saved in Lifeboat 11, but John Harper died in the cold water of the Atlantic Ocean and his body was never recovered. The events recorded in this book of Mr Harper calling for 'women, children and unbelievers to the lifeboats' are based on eye witness accounts of survivors of the sinking. The account of the man trusting the Lord Jesus as a result of Mr Harper's words whilst swimming in the sea, are also factual, having been recorded by the man himself, who survived the tragedy, and testified to this incident at a meeting of survivors, four years after the ship's sinking.

Postscript for Nana Harper

A week after arriving in New York, young Jessica Annie Harper (Nana) returned to England and was brought up in Scotland by her uncles (her father's brothers) and their respective families. Nana, eventually, married Reverend Pont of St John's Rectory in Moffat, Dumfries-shire. Nana did not speak about the tragedy until her later years, when she started to keep in touch with other survivors, notably Eva Hart (Harrison). She passed away on Thursday, 10th April 1986, exactly seventy-four years to the day of the *Titanic's* departure from Southampton.

Whilst the *Titanic* was collecting passengers in Queenstown, a famous picture of the ship was taken from behind the fourth funnel looking forward along the second class promenade deck, on the starboard side of the ship. This photograph shows a man in a long dark coat and wearing a hat, holding the hand of a small girl who appears to be skipping. It is commonly assumed that the two in this picture are John Harper and his daughter, Nana.

John Harper Timeline

1872   John Harper born on Wednesday, 29th May.

1886   John Harper trusted the Lord Jesus as his Saviour on Sunday, 28th March.

1899   Bruce Ismay becomes chairman of White Star Line who will build the *Titanic*.

1901   Queen Victoria dies on 22nd January, aged 81, having reigned as Queen for 63 years.

1906   Annie Jessie Harper (Nana) born on Monday, 1st January, 1906.

1909   On 31st March, work commences on building the *Titanic* in Belfast.

1910   King Edward VII dies on 6th May.

1911   On 31st May, over 100,000 people watch the *Titanic* being launched in Belfast.

1911   King George V crowned King on 22nd June.

1912   On 2nd April, the *Titanic* undergoes sea trials in Belfast Lough before setting sail for Southampton.

1912   The *Titanic* arrives in Southampton on 3rd April, following an uneventful 570 mile trip from Belfast.

1912   The *Titanic* sets sail on her maiden voyage on Wednesday, 10th April.

1912   Sunday, 14th April, the *Titanic* strikes an iceberg at 11.40 p.m., having travelled about 2000 miles in total.

1912   Monday, 15th at 12.45 a.m., the first lifeboat (No 7) leaves the the *Titanic*.

1912   Monday 15th at 2.05 a.m., the last lifeboat leaves the *Titanic*.

1912   Monday 15th at 2.20 a.m., the *Titanic* sinks below the Atlantic Ocean.

1912   Monday 15th, John Harper seen swimming in the
       water urging people to place their trust in the
       Lord Jesus.

1912   Monday 15th, at 4:10 a.m., rescue ship *Carpathia*
       arrives at scene of sinking and commences to
       rescue survivors in lifeboats.

1912   *Carpathia* arrives in New York on 18th April at
       8:00 p.m. carrying 705 survivors.

1914   First World War commences on 28th July.

1918   First World War ends on 11th November
       (Armistice day).

1939   Second World War commences on 1st September.

1945   Second World War ends on 2nd September.

1955   American author Walter Lord publishes his book
       'A Night to Remember' based on his interviews
       with many *Titanic* survivors. This book is regarded
       as the book that commenced the world's interest in
       the *Titanic* disaster.

1958   The black and white film version of the sinking of
       the *Titanic* called 'A Night to Remember'
       is released staring British actor Kenneth More
       as 2nd Officer Lightoller.

1985   Dr Robert Ballard discovers the *Titanic* wreck
       in two main parts lying at a depth of 12,460 feet
       (3797 metres).

1986   Nana Harper dies on Thursday, 10th April.

Take Five Minutes

What is the most important thing in your life?

From the age of thirteen, John Harper had only one real ambition in life – to point people to the Lord Jesus Christ as Saviour and Lord. This great desire led him, aged just eighteen, to one of the neediest areas of Glasgow at that time. Here, he began to preach and tell the wonderful story of Jesus and his love. Later in his ministry, he was called by God to serve him in a similar way in London. In everything that John Harper did, the will of God and desire to serve the Lord were the most important things in his life.

What do we consider to be of the greatest importance in our lives? Although examinations, education, relationships and job prospects are all vitally important, the Bible does state that we only obtain real satisfaction when we serve the Lord fully. Are you prepared to place the Lord Jesus as number one in your life, so that you will seek his guidance and will in everything you do? Then, as with John Harper, you will be able to bring glory and pleasure to God even in life's greatest trials!

Bible Study 1

Look up the following passages
  Exodus 20:3
  Matthew 6:33 – 34

What important thing do these verses tell us that God wants to be in our life? What legitimate things can you think of that stop us placing God as number one in our life? Think about ways you can make God the centre of your life and how this will affect your other important issues.

  Read 1 Samuel 2:30

The nation of Israel had failed to place God first in their national life. However, despite this God promises in this verse, 'Them that honour me I will honour.' Think about what this means for you. What does God promise to do if you put him first in your life?

Take Five Minutes

How was Mr Harper able and willing to speak to so many people about the Lord Jesus?

It is not always easy to speak up for the Lord Jesus. Mr Harper sought again and again to tell people of the Lord Jesus. What gave him the courage and strength to do this, even to some of the most important and influential people he met in his life?

The moment he was saved at thirteen years of age, John Harper was indwelt by God's Holy Spirit. It is the Holy Spirit who can make us bold to speak up, not only for the Lord Jesus, but against that which we know to be wrong. One of the Holy Spirit's works is to convict men of sin. That is what he did to John Flynn (see page 126), through the Word of God. Sometimes we can feel bad about something we know we have done wrong in our life, especially after we have read the Bible. This is most probably the Holy Spirit convicting us of our sin and urging us to trust the Lord Jesus as our Saviour. Once we do that, He seeks to make us more like the Lord Jesus, as we read the Bible and seek to follow its teachings.

Bible Study 2

Read the following verses about the Holy Spirit
    John 14:26
    Acts 1:8

Think of three things these two passages tell us the Holy Spirit (called here the Holy Ghost) will help us to do. What other word does the Lord Jesus use to describe the Holy Spirit in John 14:26. Why do you think the Holy Spirit is given this name? In Acts 1:8, who does the Holy Spirit help us to witness for?

Why do you think God has given Christians the Holy Spirit? How do you think the fact that he lives in us, should help us to walk and live for Christ? In Ephesians 4:30 we are told to, 'grieve not the Holy Spirit of God'. Can you think of some ways that you can grieve the Holy Spirit? What do you think is the best way to avoid doing things that grieve him?

Take Five Minutes

Why was the loss of Mr Harper's New Testament such an important thing to him?

Although this incident is not based on fact, it was placed in the story to try and show John Harper's great interest and love for the Word of God. Many Christians have Bibles and New Testaments that they have had and used for many years, and they know just where to look for certain verses when using them. Some also underline what they consider to be key verses or passages, so that they can refer more easily to them when next reading that part of the Bible. Do you read any part of the Bible? A good habit is to read a portion every day, asking God to help you understand what you read. Try to use the same Bible so that its pages and layout become familiar to you as you read it. It will take time, but eventually you will remember not only where passages are in the Bible (as Mr Harper was able to point out to Mr Flynn), but also where on the page they are.

Bible Study 3

Read Psalm 119: 9-16

Once you have read this passage from the longest Psalm in the Bible, see how many words the writer uses to describe the Word of God? Think of at least three positive things that the Psalmist says he will do with the Bible. What were some of the results of the writer's interest in the Word of the Lord?

The whole Psalm is full of references to the Word of God and a good exercise would be to read all 178 verses, underlining each mention of God's Word. In verse 11, the writer states that he has hidden God's Word in his heart so that he will not sin against God. What do you think he means and how will this help him to avoid sinning?

Take Five Minutes

Mr Harper was known as a man of prayer. What is prayer and why is it so important?

Throughout this account of Mr Harper's life on board the *Titanic,* there are many references to him praying or having prayed for something specific. He prayed for safety on the journey to the ship, he prayed at Nana's bedside each night and he prayed once he knew the ship was in great danger. Prayer is a wonderful resource that God has given to Christians to enable them to speak to him about anything. It is not, however, to be used for selfish ideas about, for example, getting rich or wanting your favourite sports team to win. It is to help us in seeking out God's will for us, in our life and service. In prayer, we should praise God's name for who he is and what he has done for us. That will bring glory to his name and strengthen our own hearts. You will notice that Mr Harper was always praying for others and their needs before his own wants and desires.

Bible Study 4

Read 1 Timothy 2: 1-10

In this passage the apostle Paul is giving some instruction with regards to how to pray and what to pray for. In the first verse how many different words does Paul use to describe prayer? What do you think each of these words mean and how do you think they differ from each other?

In verse 2 Paul instructs us to pray for all in authority. Make a list of all the people you think that this may include, then consider what you could ask God in prayer in relation to each person on your list. Think about what is said in the last part of the verse about leading a quiet and peaceable life. How do you think that your prayers for the people on your list could bring this about?

Take Five Minutes

Why do you think God allowed Nana and her father to board the *Titanic* when he knew what was going to happen to it?

There is no getting around it; this is a difficult question to answer! Maybe the verse Nana remembered in the last chapter of the story that, 'all things work together for good to them that love God,' is as close as we can get to fully understanding or appreciating why God allowed these events. We know from eyewitness accounts of how Mr Harper tried to point desperate people to the Lord Jesus as Saviour, as the *Titanic* was sinking. Maybe many, through hearing his witness to the Lord Jesus, repented and trusted Christ as Saviour in the last minutes of their lives.

Bible Study 5

Read 2nd Corinthians 1:3-4

What two titles does Paul give to God at the close of verse 3? Why do you think Paul recognises God by these names? Can you think of some ways that God could show His mercies and comfort in your life?

In verse 4, the writer tells us that God comforts us in all our tribulations or trials. Whatever trial, problem or difficulties we face, God is more than able to meet them if we tell him about them and let him help us. This verse also tells us why God allows problems and trials in our lives. It is in order to strengthen our faith, which enables us to help others when they are going through similar circumstances. If you are a Christian, can you think of trials God has helped you through? How will this assist you in helping others?

Torchbearers Series

Polycarp: The Crown of Fire
by William C Newson
ISBN 978-1-84550-041-2

Danger on the Hill
by Catherine Mackenzie
ISBN 978-1-85792-784-9

Jim Elliot: He is no Fool
by Irene Howat
ISBN 978-1-84550-064-1

James Chalmers: The Rainmaker's Friend
by Irene Howat
ISBN 978-1-84550-154-9

William Tyndale: The Smuggler's Flame
by Lori Rich
ISBN 978-1-85792-972-0

The Adventures Series

African Adventures by Dick Anderson
ISBN 978-1-85792-807-5

Amazon Adventures by Horace Banner
ISBN 978-1-85792-440-4

Cambodian Adventures by Donna Vann
ISBN 978-1-84550-474-8

Great Barrier Reef Adventures by Jim Cromarty
ISBN 978-1-84550-068-9

Himalayan Adventures by Penny Reeve
ISBN 978-1-84550-080-1

Kiwi Adventures by Bartha Hill
ISBN 978-1-84550-282-9

New York City Adventures by Donna Vann
ISBN 978-1-84550-546-2

Outback Adventures by Jim Cromarty
ISBN 978-1-85792-974-4

Pacific Adventures by Jim Cromarty
ISBN 978-1-84550-475-5

Rainforest Adventures by Horace Banner
ISBN 978-1-85792-627-9

Rocky Mountain Adventures by Betty Swinford
ISBN 978-1-85792-962-1

Scottish Highland Adventures
by Catherine Mackenzie
ISBN 978-1-84550-281-2

Wild West Adventures by Donna Vann
ISBN 978-1-84550-065-8

TRAILBLAZER SERIES

Gladys Aylward, No Mountain too High
ISBN 978-1-85792-594-4

Corrie ten Boom, The Watchmaker's Daughter
ISBN 978-1-85792-116-8

David Brainerd, A Love for the Lost
ISBN 978-1-84550-695-7

Paul Brand, The Shoes that Love Made
ISBN 978-1-84550-630-8

Bill Bright, Dare to be Different
ISBN 978-1-85792-945-4

John Bunyan, The Journey of a Pilgrim
ISBN 978-1-84550-458-8

Amy Carmichael, Rescuer by Night
ISBN 978-1-85792-946-1

John Calvin, After Darkness Light
ISBN 978-1-84550-084-9

Jonathan Edwards, America's Genius
ISBN 978-1-84550-329-1

Michael Faraday, Spiritual Dynamo
ISBN 978-1-84550-156-3

Billy Graham, Just Get Up Out Of Your Seat
ISBN 978-1-84550-095-5

Adoniram Judson, Danger on the Streets of Gold
ISBN 978-1-85792-660-6

Isobel Kuhn, Lights in Lisuland
ISBN 978-1-85792-610-1

C.S. Lewis, The Storyteller
ISBN 978-1-85792-487-9

Eric Liddell, Finish the Race
ISBN 978-1-84550-590-5

CHRISTIAN FOCUS PUBLICATIONS

Christian Focus | Christian Heritage | CF4K | Mentor

Christian Focus Publications publishes books for adults and children under its four main imprints: Christian Focus, Christian Heritage, CF4K and Mentor. Our books reflect that God's word is reliable and Jesus is the way to know him, and live for ever with him.

Our children's publication list includes a Sunday school curriculum that covers pre-school to early teens; puzzle and activity books. We also publish personal and family devotional titles, biographies and inspirational stories that children will love.

If you are looking for quality Bible teaching for children then we have an excellent range of Bible story and age specific theological books.

From pre-school to teenage fiction, we have it covered!

Find us at our web page:
www.christianfocus.com

CF4 •K
Because you're never too young to know Jesus